ONLY
PACK
WHAT YOU CAN
CARRY

ONLY
PACK
WHAT YOU CAN
CARRY

My Path to Inner Strength,

Confidence, and True Self-Knowledge

Janice Holly Booth

NATIONAL GEOGRAPHIC

WASHINGTON, D.C.

Published by the National Geographic Society

1145 17th Street N.W., Washington, D.C. 20036

Library of Congress Cataloging-in-Publication Data
Booth, Janice.
Only pack what you can carry : my path to inner strength, confidence, and true self knowledge / Janice Holly Booth.
    p. cm.
ISBN 978-1-4262-0733-4 (hardcover)
1. Voyages and travels. 2. Booth, Janice--Travel. 3. Self-actualization (Psychology) I. Title.
G465.B659 2011
910.4--dc22

                        2010045500

Photo page 263: Courtesy of Cross Country International

The National Geographic Society is one of the world's largest nonprofit scientific and educational organizations. Founded in 1888 to "increase and diffuse geographic knowledge," the Society works to inspire people to care about the planet. It reaches more than 375 million people worldwide each month through its official journal, *National Geographic,* and other magazines; National Geographic Channel; television documentaries; music; radio; films; books; DVDs; maps; exhibitions; live events; school publishing programs; interactive media; and merchandise. National Geographic has funded more than 9,200 scientific research, conservation and exploration projects and supports an education program promoting geographic literacy.

For more information, please call 1-800-NGS LINE (647-5463) or write to the following address:

National Geographic Society
1145 17th Street N.W.
Washington, D.C. 20036-4688 U.S.A.

Visit us online at www.nationalgeographic.com

For information about special discounts for bulk purchases, please contact
National Geographic Books Special Sales: ngspecsales@ngs.org

For rights or permissions inquiries, please contact National Geographic Books
Subsidiary Rights: ngbookrights@ngs.org

Interior design: Cameron Zotter

Printed in the United States of America

10/QGF-CML/1

To my parents
Katrina Steve Kachuk and Roy Leonard Booth

CONTENTS

ONLY
PACK
WHAT YOU CAN
CARRY

CHAPTER ONE

BAGGAGE

*If you want to realize your potential, if you want to know
what really matters to you . . . you need to take time to think
about things deep in that place where you tell the truth.*

ALL I EVER WANTED WAS A HORSE. No husband, children, or white picket fence for me: While other girls were doo-
dling their initials and imagining how their married names would
look, I was drawing wild-at-heart horses with flowing manes
and nostrils ringed with fire. My father hung a chalkboard in the
basement where I drew equine stories—herds crossing the plains;
mares and foals galloping wild; unicorns. When I was ten and
there wasn't a square inch of the house that hadn't been defaced
by a horse doodle, my parents relented and bought me one. His
name was Rocky—flatfooted, Roman-nosed, pig-eyed, and mule-
eared, with epic dandruff and a bad disposition. We brought him
home in my father's work van, shoved in there like an old, overstuffed couch picked up at a flea market. My dad struck a hard
bargain—we paid all of one dollar for this creature, leading me

to wonder (much later, of course) whether he was actually a horse at all and not some kind of barnyard experiment gone awry: a horse crossed with a cow crossed with a donkey crossed with an emu. But young girls are easily overcome by fairy tales, and Rocky to me was nothing less than every one of the gallant steeds I had been faithfully beckoning into my life, via my drawings, since I first picked up a pencil.

I was a tiny little thing—all knobby knees and elbows, skinny and straight, freckled, with long black hair and cat's-eye glasses. My parents had to pinch pennies, which meant I wore my older sister's hand-me-down clothes, often until I had not only outgrown them but split the seams. "Flood Pants" was my middle name, and it became easier to spend all my time on horseback, exploring my little corner of the world, than to be around mean people.

I grew up just outside Vancouver before it became a metropolis. Back then the area had miles of woods, streams, mountains, and fields to ride through. Dad could afford to pay a dollar for Rocky but not the hundred or so for a saddle, which meant I rode bareback for a long time. Up until the point Rocky was delivered into my life I was shy, quiet, and compliant. But he was so disobedient and conniving, I had to learn how to be authoritative and commanding. I had to become a presence that couldn't be ignored. Until Rocky, I never swore. Until Rocky, I never felt a violent thought. Until Rocky, I was a doormat. Teaching that horse who was boss—me, about as big as a golf pencil—took all the determination I had. That horse bucked me off every chance he got. He found every low-hanging branch in our little corner of British Columbia and headed for it at a dead run, literally leaving me hanging while he galloped away. He'd pretend to be lame, and when I'd dismount to check his hoof for stones, he'd run off, tail high in the air, farting as he galloped toward home and the grain bucket.

Oh, how I cursed that horse. Oh, how I loved him. But I didn't love him for him. I loved him for the freedom and power I felt when I could gallop through a meadow, sneak up on deer or pheasants, jump big ditches, and ride down steep embankments to wade in cool, shaded streams. On horseback, I could go places and see things I couldn't on foot. I could cover miles and miles of wilderness. The whole world looked different from the back of my horse.

Rocky finally took seriously my efforts to dominate him, and our time together became a little more tranquil. He succumbed to my will and the threat of the whip, but despite the external peacefulness, some ember of determination still glowed inside me, yearning for a whiff of controversy to feed the flame. I started to speak out in class. It suddenly seemed completely ridiculous that girls were not allowed to wear pants to school—even in winter, when we had to navigate snowdrifts in dresses and rubber boots. We weren't allowed to wear panty hose either. What was this nonsense? I asked the principal, Mr. Toole.

Mr. Toole, with his big, square, black-rimmed glasses that looked like twin TV sets, said, "Janice, if you can get the majority of the girls in your class to sign a petition, I will allow you and them to wear pants." He said this to me then smiled. I thought, *This is too easy. You are a* fool, *Mr. Toole! This thing will be knocked out by the end of week*. I was in fifth grade.

That night, with the help of my dad, I created a petition. It simply said, "We, the undersigned, wish to be granted the right to wear pants to school." I thought there couldn't be a simpler thing.

All the girls wanted to wear pants. All the girls complained about having to wear dresses. All I had to do to change that was round up a posse and have them sign their names.

I was about to get my first lesson in reality.

Mr. Toole had the benefit of wisdom and cynicism on his side. He watched with a bemused grin as I was rejected, one after another, by every girl in my class. I was at once outraged, perplexed, and crushed that no one would support what I thought was a group cause.

"But don't you want to wear pants to school?" I pleaded with Joan White.

"Of course I do," she answered, "but I'll get in trouble if I sign that thing." Girls weren't supposed to assert themselves back then or get involved in any sort of "controversy," which apparently my pants petition was. Some girls wouldn't speak to me at all that day. I went home defeated.

"Don't give up," Dad told me. "Go back and try a different approach." I thought about what had worked with Rocky. The next day I approached the girls in my class.

"Sign this," I told them, brandishing the pen like a whip, "or you don't want to even *think* about what will happen."

The whip proved once again victorious, and with the majority of the girls' names on my petition, I knocked on Mr. Toole's door. "Here it is," I told him when he ushered me inside. "We will start wearing pants tomorrow."

"Janice," he said, tossing the petition into the garbage without giving it a glance, "you can come to school in a bathing suit, you can come to school naked, but you will never, *ever* come to school in pants."

"But what about . . . ?" I pleaded, pointing at the wastebasket.

"I repeat," he said, bringing his big, fat face close to mine. He paused for effect and I watched my reflection in his glasses, my face turning a furious red. "You will *never* come to school in pants."

I staggered out of his office and stood in the hallway. What just happened? I'd followed the rules, but it was all a trick. The injustice! There was no going back to class now, only to admit to failure. Were adults really so treacherous and full of deceit? Was I completely naive? I'd done everything I was supposed to do, and therefore, the fair thing was that I should have won this round. It was only because I was a child and powerless that I was about to be humiliated and shamed into submission.

The next day, careful not to reveal my plan to my mother, I wore a bathing suit under my dress, and when I arrived at school I disrobed. The principal was summoned to our class and, gasping, ordered me to "put some clothes on, for God's sake!" My mother was called to Mr. Toole's office on "an emergency basis," and after he related my "insubordination," I was placed on suspension. In his office, in front of my mother, I confronted him.

"But you told me I could come to school in a bathing suit or naked."

"I said no such thing," he bellowed.

"Mr. Toole," I said, "you're lying."

It was a while before I saw the inside of my classroom again.

Two years later Mr. Toole was transferred, and girls were finally allowed to wear pants.

IN HIGH SCHOOL, my body shape morphed from the straight and skinny golf pencil to a classic hourglass, and I wore my skirts as short as I could get away with because the rule was that skirts had to come to the knee. I talked back to teachers. I cut class whenever I could. My grades were fine; I just couldn't stand to be around what I felt was the hypocrisy of the adult world. The harder I tried to distance myself from it, the more they tried to pull me back in. Each year I became more and more sullen, counting the days before graduation and freedom. My parents were at their wits' end. Was it so much to ask that everyone just leave me alone? My only salvation was the time I spent riding Rocky in the mountains after school.

Then came the infamous science experiment where I refused to dissect a pig because I didn't want to participate in what I believed was a wasteful and unnecessary killing of animals.

"I'll do three times the requirements on another project," I told my teacher. It was an equitable proposal, I thought: The school would respect my position and I would do extra work, but the adult agenda was much different. I came home from school to find that the school counselor and my parents had conspired to teach me a lesson.

Rocky was gone.

"We gave him away," my mother said, satisfied that this punishment would finally elicit a response. "You did this to yourself. You don't deserve a horse."

That was the last nail in the coffin, sealing away any hope or chance I had to trust or respect adults or authority. My horse had been the only thing that kept me from going over to the dark side. Those after-school rides were critical interventions, distracting me from drugs, from drinking, from true badness. After I could no longer ride the trails, I went down many wrong roads and am forever grateful—through whatever grace granted me from the universe—that I didn't end up behind bars. Or worse.

Freedom could not come soon enough, and when graduation ceremonies concluded, I vowed never to go back to school again.

Freed from school and its aggravations, I left home and took any job I could get just so I could afford to live away from my parents' house. I worked as an administrative assistant, as a meter reader, then as manager of a recreation center. There was nothing wrong with the work I was doing, but I was bored. Where was the balance between a paycheck and engagement?

Then, an opportunity to work in the court system presented itself. Two weeks later, I was sitting in a courtroom, recording evidence in a murder trial. Quickly, I felt a love-hate tug-of-war with the work. Some of the cases were really exciting and every day was different. But I was also seeing the worst in people and that was no good for even deeply cynical me. I knew that the teens coming through the system were walking a tightrope over a critical chasm. What they said to the judge mattered. If they could convince the courtroom that they were worth one last chance, they usually got it. But if they were sullen and churlish, the way I'd been, they were sent to juvenile detention. If there'd ever been hope of a real future for them, it flew away at that moment, fast and forever, like a helium balloon released from a child's hand.

I had narrowly escaped that fate myself. My big crime had been that I'd been rebellious and outspoken, and that had earned me the "bad kid" label. After a while, I had started to live up to that label. Why not? It wasn't as if anyone was giving me the benefit of the doubt.

Right around this time I began to study creative writing at night in the college next to the courthouse, and I found some release in taking shards of facts and creating mosaics of fiction. Being a court recorder was a great job for an aspiring writer. The stories behind the headlines—murder, kidnapping, and rape, along with the mundane but sometimes fascinating details behind serial shoplifting and drunk and disorderly charges—were always different. I began to realize that in almost every single criminal trial, the one consistent thing that had unraveled the carefully constructed plots of the accused was that someone spoke a secret. It was almost as if they were compelled to. How hard is it, I wondered, to just keep your mouth shut? I took a lesson from court: Keep your secrets to yourself. This was another way for me to stay safe in the world. If I never told my secrets, no one could find the key to my vulnerability, and therefore, I reasoned, they could never hurt me.

So, court represented my exterior scaffolding, but behind the scenes I was busy doing what twentysomethings do, partying almost every night until 3 or 4 a.m., then making valiant attempts to stay awake at work. More than once I fell asleep in the middle of a trial and had to ask for evidence to be repeated. On weekends my boyfriend and I were chasing his passion for exploring rivers via raft. I saw places in British Columbia and northern Washington State probably seen by very few, because the only way to get to them was tortuous, difficult, and only achievable by raft or kayak. I loved the thrill, too, of smashing through roaring, churning, insane water, the chaos of it completely overwhelming, the moments in the rapids expanding time to make every minute seem like ten.

Then came the fateful day we chose the wrong river. My boyfriend was ambitious; he wanted to build a résumé of white-water firsts, and the upper Tulameen River in British Columbia had never been successfully paddled. He studied the topographic maps, and we did some preliminary scouting. All evidence pointed to the fact that this section of the river was unnavigable. That didn't stop us. The locals in the area swore there were several waterfalls along the route, but when we offered them cash if they would drive us— the two of us and two paddling companions—and our equipment to our intended put-in spot up-canyon, they agreed.

The river was in flood stage, and right from the start there were problems. The two other paddlers were stationed in the front of the raft, but the force of the water snapped their wooden paddles in half before we'd gone even a mile. My boyfriend had had the presence of mind to strap in his oar frame, and once the river had us in its torrent, he spent all his time back paddling to slow and turn the boat, but it was no use. The river was too swollen, the canyon too narrow, there were no eddies, no quiet places to pull over and regroup. I was in the back, bailing water as if I were trying to put out a fire. The other two paddlers, no longer able to help, simply watched with trepidation as we slammed around every curve.

Suddenly the river became wide, shallow, and slow. Calm even. We stopped to organize our thoughts and bail every last drop of river water out of the raft. We looked all around at the canyon, wondering if we could portage or even climb up the steep sides of the rock walls, to avoid what lay ahead. It was impossible. The canyon was sheer on one side and steep and choked with trees and rock outcroppings on the other. My boyfriend gave assignments should the river become aggressive again, and we reluctantly pushed off, unsure of what waited for us downstream. The pleasant floating on the wide, flat water lasted only a minute or two. A roaring sound, muffled at first, grew louder and clearer as we approached a turn.

"What's that noise?" I asked, as the raft floated around the corner.

"Waterfall!" shouted one of the paddlers in front. Instantly the canyon narrowed like two hands clapping together, the river swelling and pushing us to where the water disappeared over a sheer edge, mist floating up into the air above.

My boyfriend back paddled with every molecule of resolve he had, but it was as if we were being pulled along by a cable, and fast. The shore was within reach, but the floodwaters had risen above the shoreline boulders that might have sheltered us from the current. Tree branches brushed the surface of the crazy water, and I grabbed at some to slow us down, resulting in deep cuts and lost fingernails. I looked ahead and there it was, the edge of the waterfall. We were racing toward it. In the time it took to say two words, we would be hurtled over the edge.

My boyfriend jammed an oar in between two rocks, and it slowed the raft just long enough for all of us to jump out. Without a word, we separated, each of us finding a little spot to ourselves and sitting in silence for a while. We'd managed to save ourselves from certain death, but we still had to get out of this wild and undeveloped canyon. I'd been convinced that this was the moment of my death, and it nearly was. At that point I'd been rafting for a good three years.

I didn't know it then, but that would be the last time I ever went on the river. That was the very first door that fear closed inside my heart, quietly. I never heard it happen.

My boyfriend eventually started a white-water rafting busi-ness—on well-researched though challenging routes. Although I refused to raft anymore, I made myself useful by being an action photographer, driving the recovery vehicle—usually a big, ugly, beat-up white work van with questionable brakes—to the take-out spot, stopping at least five or six times along the route to take pictures. Sometimes when the raft was making its way through a narrow canyon, I'd tie a rope around my waist and the other end to the bumper of the van, and hang off the side of a cliff to get a good action picture of the rafters. It was ridiculously dangerous, but back then I would do anything for a shot.

One morning I woke up scratching two little welts that looked like mosquito bites on the inside of my wrist. Within an hour my hand and wrist had swollen to three times their normal size and the pain was unbearable. A few hours later, the same thing hap-pened to my face, my eyes swelling so badly I couldn't see. Then my ankles puffed up and I couldn't walk. A call to the doctor resulted in an admonishment to take antihistamines. After ingest-ing five times the suggested dosage, the swelling subsided, but I was black and blue in all the places I'd been swollen, my face looking as though it had been used as a punching bag. Every day it got worse. The same swelling and receding must have been happen-ing internally as well, because I couldn't eat and my five-foot-six frame withered to less than 100 pounds.

My boyfriend took care of me—carrying me from the kitchen to the bedroom or wherever I needed to move, bringing me water, staying up with me at night when I couldn't sleep, letting me cry and cry and cry. But he didn't want us to be seen together in public because he was worried that people would think he'd been beating me. Three different doctors couldn't diagnose me. And none of them would give me anything except allergy medicine. Some days I would have minor welts and intense itching and other days I couldn't walk. My joints would swell so large I thought the skin would split. Late at night, when the pain drove me to tears, I'd fill the bathtub with scalding water and plunge into it, the burning sensation a distraction from the pain of the swelling. It was the first and only time in my life I considered suicide, just to get away from the suffering. I was 24 years old.

One night I staggered into the bathroom to run my swollen wrists under cold water. In the mirror, I saw everything turn to black and white, like an x-ray. Both knees started to knock—I heard them banging against the cabinet under the sink. Thrusting both arms out to steady myself—like pushing two walls apart—I felt something reach deep inside me and start to yank at my soul. It was the first time I felt my life going away. I knew if I let that invisible hand have its way, I would collapse on the floor and be dead. Sweat ran down my body as if I were standing in the rain. In what was likely only seconds but felt like forever, my vision returned, my legs found their strength, and I was OK. Many years later, I read something by Ernest Hemingway, describing death pulling at his insides like a handkerchief. I'm here to tell you, that's *exactly* how it feels.

Finally, after being sent to a psychiatrist to ensure I wasn't making the whole thing up, my doctor reluctantly prescribed steroids to complement the excessive dosage of antihistamines. Symptoms had a firm hold on me at this point and the steroids barely made a dent, but they did keep things from getting any worse. And then, three agonizing months later, as mysteriously as the affliction appeared, it disappeared. I still didn't have a diagnosis. But I no longer trusted my body. Or doctors.

While sick, I'd had to take a leave of absence from work. Housebound, I read voraciously. Because I was so weak and in constant discomfort, riding was now out of the question, but I'd gaze longingly at brochures for exotic equestrian travel vacations. Italy, France, Ireland, and Scotland all looked wonderful, but one image kept seducing me: a picture of a blond, tanned woman galloping on a white horse in the blue Costa Rican surf. The first time I saw it I said out loud, "I want to be her." Even then, it seemed a strange thing to say. "I want to go there," or "I want to do that," would have been more appropriate. I'd revisit that image several times a year, just to look at it and repeat that strange phrase over and over again in my mind: *I want to be her.*

When I wasn't dreaming about riding horses in Central America and when I could clear my head enough to focus, I worked on writing. A former writing professor from my after-work college fiction-writing classes suggested I apply for a fellowship to the Banff School of the Arts. He thought it would be a good place for me to spend an intensive six weeks working on nothing but writing. I put together a portfolio and applied. To my surprise and delight, I was accepted, with a full scholarship. Healthy now, I asked to extend my leave of absence from work so I could go to Banff. My beloved '69 Chevy Nova—with a three-on-the-tree gear shift, a floor completely rusted through, and all the shaky parts held together partly by electrical tape—groaned under the weight of suitcases, boxes, paper, and a typewriter but carried me reliably from Vancouver all through the steep and scenic Fraser River Canyon, across the border into southern Alberta and the majestic Canadian Rockies.

Six weeks in that spectacular location, coupled with the fact that my only obligation was to write and give feedback to other writers, was a gift of inestimable value. The surroundings were the antithesis of the courtroom, with its stark walls, witness stands, and prisoner docks. In Banff, the natural setting swept toward the jagged mountain peaks and deep blue ranges topped with snow. And the people were talented and brilliant; through their art, they were adding value to the community of man, not diminishing it.

Banff had long been known as an international center for art and culture, and I met artists from many countries and in every discipline—dance, music, the visual arts, architecture, electronic art. I'd found the right environment at last, one where I could be myself and speak my voice without someone trying to quash it. And that experience helped me decide what I didn't want in life. I didn't want to be surrounded any longer by drama, death, and despicable people. If I remained working in court, I'd lose some part of myself to apathy, because that would become my only defense against the violence and ugliness I was seeing every day.

While at Banff, I was offered the chance to run a music festival in Buffalo, New York, and knew I had to take it. I went back home, quit my job, sold everything or gave it away, announced to friends and family that I was leaving, and in no time, I was on a plane headed east. It was only then that a little voice asked, *Are you sure you know what you're doing?* It was the first time I'd actually wondered if I was making a huge mistake. *I can always go back,* I assured myself.

Buffalo was no Vancouver, the waterfront a visual catastrophe of rusting grain elevators and abandoned steel mills, but it was summer and warm in a way I'd never felt back home. As long as the sun was shining and I could be outdoors, any homesickness or second-guessing my decision stayed buried.

The music festival came and went, then autumn arrived, the blazing fall foliage unlike anything I'd seen on the West Coast. Before long I was engaged to a local composer and thrust into a life surrounded by academics and celebrities. I met people like Yo-Yo Ma and Philip Glass and attended parties with well-known singers, musicians, choreographers, dancers, and others. But it was not their fame that intrigued me—it was how they saw the world with a lens of experience much greater than mine—and how they translated that view through their art. It was a very different world from criminal court and white-water rafting and I could feel my sensibilities morphing into something different.

When the first snowflakes fell, I watched from inside our apartment as they swirled gently in the darkness. *How pretty,* I thought, donning my best and most trustworthy Canadian winter jacket. I walked outside and immediately turned and walked back in. The wind had cut through me like a knife. It would have been warmer to plunge my face into a bucket of ice. And winter had just begun.

Buffalo presented a winter environment more brutal than anything I'd known, so I spent a lot of time indoors, alone, thinking about my new life in the United States. My fiancé's colleagues and friends couldn't have been more welcoming and supportive, but I needed my own friends and my own sphere of influence. Riding horses, I decided, also had to become part of my life again; there was a big, gaping hole where it was missing. My fiancé agreed, so I contracted myself out as a trainer—riding other people's horses and getting paid for it.

This was how I ultimately met the greatest horse of my life: a big, regal, sleek, brown ex-racehorse; a Thoroughbred stallion named Lover's Reason. He'd gone lame in his right front leg after being in training to jump, and the owners needed a rider who was not intimidated by a stallion, to bring him slowly back to usefulness. Working with this massive yet skittish horse, I was touched by how careful he was, how respectful, curious, and kind, despite his enormous size and power. There was no need to rely on a whip with this horse; he was willing and eager to please.

Somewhere in his past, though, he'd been terribly abused, making him unpredictable and therefore dangerous. If I moved my hand too quickly near his head, he'd shy away, almost pulling the barn down with him, if he happened to be tied. It was as if he lived every moment *expecting* to be beaten. Despite this rather disheartening trait, his pedigree was impeccable—along the lines of Triple Crown winner Seattle Slew—so I felt lucky just to be riding him. Secretly I wondered what it would be like to own him, to rehabilitate him mentally and physically to the point where we could compete in the discipline of dressage (similar to what Lipizzaner Stallions do) and wow the world, or at least our little corner of it.

I started attending horse shows as an observer, and because horse shows can sometimes be incredibly boring, I entertained myself by photographing the competitors. Very quickly I became a sought-after equine photographer, fully booked with a weekend photography schedule from April through October. I loved that work. It was lucrative and creative, and I was making people happy.

I also became the director of readings and workshops in a literary center and began building my own network of influential and famous people. My job was to recruit ten to twelve writers to Buffalo each year for public readings, and to arrange writing workshops for the community. I also had to entertain the writers once they were in town. Every single one of them was different, some as difficult to manage as rock stars. I remember arriving at the airport to collect one of the writers, a household name. He said, "Well, you're certainly the prettiest limo driver I've ever had." Pleasant enough, but when we got to my car—a banged-up, white, two-door Toyota Corolla—he planted his feet. "I'm not getting into that thing." Apparently, he was used to having "drivers" with limousines or town cars or horse-drawn carriages, not my little white marshmallow on wheels. This is where I began to learn the fine art of negotiation. Not only did I get him into the car, I made a new friend in the process.

Between weekend photography, training horses, my job, and writing—I was fortunate to have my fiction published on a fairly regular basis in regional periodicals and literary journals—there wasn't much time for my now husband. In any event, he was busy pursuing his own career and becoming quite well known. He was also changing. What had attracted me to him, aside from his intelligence and talent, was his kindness and insight. He'd been a good listener. But with his own fame came a new and different view of the world, one I didn't share. It became easier to be away from him than to be near him, so I did what I'd always done when I wanted to distance myself from people—I rode horses and buried my nose in books or in my own writing.

Seven years into our marriage, my husband was awarded a residency at Bellagio Center, the former Villa Serbelloni, which the Rockefeller Foundation had transformed into an artists' retreat in northern Italy. I quit my job at the literary center to travel with him and live in Italy for many months. When the managers of the Villa Serbelloni learned I was a writer, they gifted me my own little studio overlooking Lago di Lecco. It was a tiny, glassed-in room that jutted out over the lake. Some afternoons, in the total peace and stillness, I'd hear beautiful chanting, like prayer, coming through the floor, as if the floorboards themselves were singing to me. I found out later that the small studio had been built over a shrine to the Virgin Mary. The praying was courtesy of the locals, who were allowed onto the property at certain times to pay their respects to the Virgin.

The time I spent in Italy, living in a virtual palace, having every need attended to, surrounded by culture and history and beauty, having no obligation but to write every day for months, was the high point in my life. Although I was only 31 years old, I recognized that time for the gift it was and never wasted or took for granted a single day or moment. On my morning walks from the villa to my little studio, through the sculpted gardens, smelling the yellow jasmine as it came into bloom, I would think how amazing it was that a girl from a struggling family in Burnaby, British Columbia, ended up here, in this indescribable place.

When it was time to leave, I cried and told the proprietors I would give up everything I had if I could just stay there. I would scrub toilets, toil in the fields, haul water from the lake . . . but they'd heard it hundreds of times before. They simply patted me on the back and showed me the door.

Reentry into American life was difficult, to say the least. I spent a good month in mourning over my separation from Italy. I tried speaking Italian to people, receiving blank stares in return. My

28

best attempts at re-creating the amazing meals we ate at the villa were sincere but disappointing. Eventually, the magical spell that had been Italy dissipated like the gray skies in Buffalo as winter turned to spring.

One bright spot was that the owners of Lover's Reason offered to sell the stallion to me—for a "modest" five-figure amount. The horse was more than worth it, but I didn't have the money and I was worried about the horse's previous fracture. We negotiated down to a four-figure amount I could live with and pay for myself, but once the prepurchase vetting process showed a fracture in the damaged leg, I retracted my offer. Now that word was out that the horse was never going to be able to compete, most potential buyers crossed him off their list. But I loved this horse and believed in his potential. Four weeks later, after some tense negotiations, this once-in-a-lifetime animal was mine for a pittance.

My husband was not pleased. Our relationship at this point was virtually nonexistent. (Even in Italy, we had more or less ignored each other.) "Just make sure I don't have to subsidize this little venture," he told me.

I hired Lover out for stud, and all his foals were beautiful and talented, leading me to the conclusion that I needed one for myself. My new dream was to breed my own version of Lover, and I began to research bloodlines and brood mares. I bought a highly pedigreed mare, Boldita, from a racing stable 20 miles away, at a bargain-basement price. Boldita and Lover had their date night, and I anxiously waited for the 11 months of gestation to pass so I could meet the new addition to the family.

Board and keep on two horses (soon to be three) would be significant, so when the owners of an equestrian center approached me and asked if I'd take over the running of it, I had to say yes, even though the equine industry is notoriously unstable. I calculated what it would save me in boarding fees, and what I could make in training and lesson fees on-site, and began an ambitious plan to turn the center into a moneymaker. The equestrian center was flourishing. I had a full complement of students and horses, and the strategic improvements and additions I'd made to the center were bringing in money. Then in December my husband took me out for my 32nd-birthday dinner and told me he wanted a divorce.

Shortly after that, I had a falling-out with the owners of the center and had to leave with one day's notice. Suddenly I'd gone from not having to pay anything to keep my horses to paying full board for both of them. The maintenance payments from my estranged husband were small, and I no longer had an income. In the divorce, the only thing I really wanted was the house. It was modest but cute. I'd found it and redecorated it, and I couldn't stand the idea of being displaced or of his living there with his girlfriend. I got the house, but I also got the mortgage payments. With little money coming in, I barely slept at night, the anxiety over losing everything making my heart pound so hard I thought it would come out of my chest.

I took temporary work at the local branch of the DuPont chemical company, working in the personnel department. Aspiring riders also contacted me, and I suddenly had a full evening and weekend schedule of students. And, with good weather ahead, the photography season would soon begin.

One cold April morning, I received a call from the owner of Boldita's barn: she'd had her foal, one month early. I left work and sped over there, the hour and a half it took me feeling like ten. There he was, a tiny, spindly-legged fuzzy brown colt with a white star in the center of his forehead and a white circle, as big as a snowball, on his muzzle. I called him Brazen, because even though he was tiny and new to the world, he didn't seem to be afraid of anything. He was playful, curious, sweet, and beautiful, just like his dad. I found that whenever I was at the barn with Brazen, brushing him, watching him cavort and run outside, my mind floated above the worries. All the stress and concern that choked me during the day and at night loosened its grip, and I was free for the few hours I was there.

It became impossible for me to afford all three horses. I came to the sad conclusion I was going to have to part with Lover. The best thing, I believed, would be to donate him to a university or college for their breeding program. It took months, but I found a respectable college with a solid veterinary and equine program, and donated him. Loading him on that trailer and closing the door ripped out a little piece of my heart.

As the trailer bumped down the road toward his new home, I saw him turn and look back. I felt like a traitor. Lover had already had to endure too many unknowns in his life, some of them really awful. I'd hoped that I'd be able to keep him from enduring any more uncertainty for the rest of his life.

He was an exceptional horse in every way, with an intuition and insight rare in horses, or people. Lover taught me patience and forgiveness, and that battles could be won with kindness instead of a whip. I felt a connection to this horse that went beyond an animal-human relationship. Deep in his eyes, there was something unique, a kind of sadness and courage I'd never seen before. It was humbling. By donating him to the veterinary college, I thought I'd done everything I could to secure a happy future for this horse who well deserved it. But two months later he was dead from a respiratory infection, the college failing to recognize and treat it in time. For years, I was so numbed by grief I couldn't even speak about it. It felt like losing a family member, and that I was the one responsible.

During this crazy time of transition, a friend was going through his own awful divorce, and we began spending time together. It didn't take long before we were practically incapable of spending any time apart. This new relationship was a powerful panacea for the hurt and betrayal that had been poisoning my waking life. Plus, he offered more than just himself: he had custody of his two very small children.

One day, while watching the little ones play outside, I reached down to scratch my ankle and immediately panicked. The affliction that had mysteriously disappeared had come back out of hiding, eight years later. I watched in horror as both ankles swelled to twice their normal size. I couldn't walk. The children ran to find their father, who carried me, hysterical, into the bedroom. It was a Saturday, but I managed to track down my new doctor and tell him what was going on.

"You've got to get me on steroids immediately," I told him, "before this thing takes hold."

"Take antihistamines until I can see you next week," he said.

"No, no, no," I wept, "you don't understand. By then it will be too late! *Please*," I pleaded, "*Please*. You don't know what I'm about to go through. Can't you just prescribe one dose-pack of Medrol for the weekend?"

"I'm not going to prescribe anything when I don't know what's going on!" he shouted. I handed the phone to my partner, but his calm attempts to reason with the doctor were no more successful. By the time the doctor could carve out time to see me, I was black and blue and every joint was swollen. My partner pushed me into the office in a wheelchair. Whether the doctor felt guilty or not, I never knew, but he referred me to two specialists and did, in fact, give me the steroids. Yet again, it was too late.

Before I saw the first specialist, my partner took pictures during the worst of my outbreaks, in case I looked relatively normal when I went to the specialist. And a good thing, too, because the day I arrived at the specialist's office, full of hope and despair, I had only two swellings—one on the inside of my knee and one on my breast. He was a young doctor, blond, pleasant. I described my symptoms. He seemed unusually interested, scooching closer on his chair as I told my tale of woe. "I have pictures," I offered, handing him the stack. He went through all of them then looked at me with a strange mix of admiration and adoration that only a freak show owner could feel toward a three-headed chicken.

"You are amazing," he said. "Do you realize we could do a whole medical conference on you? Look at this," he said, excitedly pointing at a picture of the blotches on the inside of one leg. "See how all the prostaglandin has accumulated in these dapples?" Then he paused. "Wow."

That day he took a biopsy of the swelling on my knee. I still have the scar. He wanted to punch the same kind of hole in my breast tissue but I refused. The results showed something very strange and I was referred to yet another specialist, Dr. R. By the time I saw him, I was at the end of my rope. Treatment wasn't working and no one seemed willing to help. Before I could say a single word, I burst into tears.

"The first thing we need to do," he said as he sat across from me behind his big, polished desk, "is make you comfortable. Then we'll figure out what's going on."

A ray of light might as well have come down from heaven, illuminating the halo that had popped up over his head, because this man was about to become an angel to me. Not only did he give me the correct dosage and the right medicine to make me comfortable and functional, he gave me a diagnosis: a rare blood disease, systemic not contagious, but barely known in the medical community. "Only a very few people in the world have this," he told me. "Now that we know what it is, we can keep you from ever having to go through what you've gone through." He was true to his promise. When I eventually moved to another state, Dr. R. called ahead to find another doctor capable of handling my "specialness." To this day, I cannot find the words to express how grateful I am that the universe delivered him to me.

Shortly after my divorce was final, I started to plan a celebration for my 40th birthday, six years away. I wanted to take two weeks to ride horses in the hills of Tuscany. Even with little money coming in, I made sure that every month I put $50 into a mutual fund designated solely for travel.

At home, bills were mounting; the basement was flooding, I needed a new roof, the chimney was crumbling. I couldn't make ends meet from the seasonal, unpredictable work, and anyway, at that point in my life I couldn't bear any more ambiguity. As a former director at the literary center, I'd built a good reputation in Buffalo; people trusted me and knew what I was capable of. This is how I stumbled into my first executive director position. A national arts-in-education organization, Young Audiences, was looking for someone to head its western New York chapter. The work looked fascinating and engaging, but the pay was pitiful. Still, I knew with hard work I could turn any losing proposition into a winning one. I took the job for less than I'd earned as an admin, and within a few years had increased the selection of artistic offerings and elevated the organization's status in the community. Young Audiences was awarded the National Medal of Arts by President Clinton—the first time in history the award had ever been given to an organization. I was part of a network that had made such a huge impact on youth it warranted attention from the President.

I loved this job of collaborating with artists and through art, helping to transform the lives, attitudes, and experiences of kids. But, as with most jobs in the arts, it came with no retirement plan, no health benefits, and low pay. Sadly, I realized I was going to have to consider an alternative.

I knew I wanted to stay in the nonprofit world, working in the service of children. And I wanted a career where there was no glass ceiling for women and no geographic limits. Many national nonprofits made the list: United Way; Big Brothers Big Sisters; Make-a-Wish Foundation . . . but the one that topped them all was the Girl Scouts. Well established, highly respected, international in scope, and dedicated to building strong girls and women, it seemed a perfect match for me. I sent in my résumé.

That summer, Brazen was four years old, still technically considered a colt. Horses mature slowly, and although I was riding him, I was taking it easy. I wanted to keep his legs strong and sound for a long time to come. I had taken four weeks' vacation with my partner and the children and brought Brazen to a summer cabin in the middle of nowhere, the nearest small town a good 20 miles away. Finishing up a ride one afternoon, out in a neighbor's vast hay field, Brazen spooked at a lone hay bale sitting innocently in the middle of the field. Perhaps he thought it was a bear or a crouching mountain lion, but he hopped into a hedgerow that delineated the hay field from a cow pasture next door. I kicked with my heels and tapped with the whip, and when Brazen gathered up the nerve to step back out into the hay field, he and I both heard something strange, metallic, wire on wire. He hesitated and kicked out violently with one hind leg. I looked back to see what was going on and saw that both his hind legs were tangled in an old barbed wire fence that had collapsed inside the hedgerow. Before I could make my next move, Brazen was bucking with all his might, looking and feeling like a rodeo horse trying to dislodge his rider.

All he wanted to do was get free of the biting barbed wire that had wrapped tenaciously around both hind legs, but his instincts had taken over and all bets were off. I went sailing into the air and had my right foot not got caught in the stirrup, I probably would have walked away with a broken collarbone or some other minor injury. But with my foot caught in the stirrup and Brazen bucking and pitching like the devil was on his back, my leg was torn out of the hip socket. When I hit the ground, my foot still stuck in the stirrup iron, I landed so hard that both contact lenses flew out of my eyes. I broke my jaw, a tooth, my hand, and crushed a finger. By the time my leg came free and I could get my bearings—which was within seconds—the horse was gone. Disappeared in that vast expanse of hay field. With all the adrenaline coursing through my system, I didn't feel any pain, until I tried to stand up. Where the soft tissues in my leg were no longer attached, I felt a sickening sort of grinding in my pelvis and collapsed. I tried again, and now the pain started to flood in. *Where was Brazen?* I called and listened to the silence that answered: no hoofbeats, no whinny. Disappeared.

Then I realized I needed to get help for myself. I called and called and called, hoping that my partner and the children would hear me back at the cabin. Hearing no answer, I began to crawl through more than 50 acres of hay stubble, bleeding, breathless, sick with pain, dehydrated. At one point I turned to lie on my back, telling myself to calm down, that by crying I was using the last of the water in my system. As I lay there trying to pull myself together, I saw vultures circling. It was like a really bad spaghetti Western and I actually laughed, until I started crying again. Eventually, I made it to the road and called for help again.

When the ambulance arrived, I thought the worst of the ordeal was over, but it had only begun. Brazen was missing and I was about to spend several agonizing days in the hospital. I was sure he'd been killed on the highway; I could see the gruesome accident every time I closed my eyes. But late on the first day there, after being poked, prodded, x-rayed, and moved three times to different beds (each transfer eliciting primal screams), a nurse came to me and took my hand. "Your horse," she said, her face giving nothing away, "has been found."

"He's dead, isn't he." I stated it not as a question but as a fact. She paused. "No," she answered. "I believe he's fine."

Brazen had been found cowering in the bushes near the place we were staying for the summer. Both stirrups from the saddle were missing and the reins were torn away. It would be some time before I got to see him, and when I did, the look in his eyes told me he'd been through as much anguish as I had. Physically, he seemed fine, but it was clear we were both broken, although my injuries were more tangible than his.

It was a long recovery. Several doctors told me not to ride again and to expect to walk ever after with the odd sort of waddle I adopted after the accident. I used a cane or crutches, because my mobility was so limited. I did start to ride Brazen again, but it was no longer fun. I kept expecting the next big disaster to be right around the corner.

While still on crutches, I was called for an interview with a Girl Scout council in North Carolina. I ditched the crutches for the interview but kept a cane nearby. By February 1997 I had left Buffalo for my new job as CEO of an excellent council in North Carolina, with Brazen in tow.

IN 1998 THE GIRL SCOUT COUNCIL sent me to a national conference in Utah. I decided to tack four days onto the beginning of the trip to see something I'd wanted to see since I was 17 years old: slot canyons. With a lot of physical therapy, I'd had the good fortune to recover well enough from my riding accident that I could walk again unaided, and I wanted adventure. I would fly out four days early, hike in Bryce Canyon and Zion National Parks, and visit as many slot canyons as I could. Naturally, I thought, there would be no shortage of people who would want to go with me.

And hence began my new career of traveling alone.

I was terribly naive to think that it would be easy to find some-one to fly to Utah with before a corporate meeting and spend time getting scratched and bruised, squeezing through crags and cracks, swimming in plunge pools, and navigating undulating sandstone. When I say no one would go with me, what I mean to say is that no one was even remotely interested. And not only that, everyone I approached felt it was their duty to talk me out of going in the first place.

These people—despite the fact that they didn't even know what a slot canyon was—felt compelled to try to convince me that a) it was too dangerous; b) I was crazy; c) I would be kidnapped, raped, and murdered, in that order; d) I wasn't a kid anymore and what was I thinking; and e) I would fall into a crevasse somewhere and never be heard from again. Not only that, I would be stuck down there without chocolate and other epicurean delights and was that any way to die?

I had never traveled alone before, and while the notion of it didn't frighten me, my friends were so unrelenting in their warn-ings that eventually I began to doubt the wisdom of my decision. What if they were right? What if I *was* being really naive and there were, in fact, hungry cougars and demented hikers out there ready to make a meal of me? I confess that I began to invent excuses not to go. I almost canceled several times. But ultimately I real-ized that to let this chance pass by would breed a disappointment I could not bear over time. Could I really let random, unsubstanti-ated fear diminish my capacity for risk and adventure? More and more, I realized, ever since that first rafting accident so many years ago, I had been letting fear dictate what I would or wouldn't do.

I went on that trip alone, but I didn't get to visit slot canyons. I didn't know that exploring them requires a skill called canyoneering that must be learned and practiced and one must never do it alone. And when you perch on the edge of a slot canyon, where the drop is steep and the bottom dark (if there is a bottom, who knows?), there really isn't a single part of you that says *Go for it.* So I contented myself with hiking through hoodoos and spires, up rivers and down canyons, all under the most perfectly blue sky you have ever seen. It was magnificent beyond description. My first solo trip, and I was hooked.

In December 1999 I turned 40. I had enough money in my mutual fund savings to take me to Italy, but work had become difficult and complicated and I was too nervous to leave my unruly staff unsupervised for such a long span of time. *I can go next year,* I reasoned. My partner and the children had joined me in North Carolina six months after I moved down, and I enjoyed the kids' energy and sweetness, their total devotion to bedtime stories and spending summers at the beach. But my partner was having a hard time adjusting to a new community where he had no status and no friends. Despite the promise I'd made to celebrate a birthday in Italy, I felt obligated to stay in North Carolina and help him with his adjustment.

It's hard to say exactly how it happened, but within two years of his moving in, all four of us went from being happy to being miserable. I wasn't surprised when my partner told me he and the kids were going to return to Buffalo.

On a warm morning in late August 2001, I watched them drive away. I'd expected to feel some relief—things had been really uncomfortable in the months they were packing up—but instead I felt a sickening kind of sadness, as if they had all died. It would be a while before I understood that what I was feeling was regret at losing them.

As soon as I knew my partner was serious about leaving, I had done what I'd always done—I walled myself away emotionally, because I couldn't bear to feel what I knew I should be feeling—heartbroken. I was particularly regretful that I hadn't been more interactive with the children before they left, but it was too scary. I was afraid that if I tried to say anything to them—sorry, good luck, don't forget about me—it might open up the floodgates that had been holding back years and years and years of untended emotion. Regret began to morph into guilt. I resolved to write the kids letters on a regular basis so that they would know I valued them as individuals, for themselves, not because of their connection to their father. I was determined that they would not feel they had lost yet another mother.

On September 10, 2001, two weeks after they left, I woke up and felt a grapefruit-size protrusion in my abdomen and made an appointment for my doctor to see me on September 13. I was trying to stay calm but couldn't shake the feeling that my strange blood disorder had warped into something more sinister. With the compounded grief and uncertainty of my life, it was taking everything I had to hold myself together.

The next day was September 11. When the first tower fell, the same thing happened inside me—something long-standing and carefully constructed collapsed into a heap of rubble. While the second tower burned, I whispered over and over, "Hang on, hang on," as much to myself as to the building and the people in it. I knew if that second tower fell, the thing teetering inside of me would too. When Tower One collapsed, whatever steel beams had been girding the life I'd created for myself—keeping people and emotions at arm's length—became as twisted and wrecked as what now remained of the World Trade Center.

Then I started to cry and couldn't stop for three months.

In October, an ultrasound of my abdomen revealed two tumors that might or might not be malignant. The doctor wanted to operate as soon as possible, but I had a hiking trip planned for May and reasoned that if the tumors weren't malignant, it didn't matter if I waited. If they were, then there was a good chance I wouldn't be hiking again for a long time, if ever. Reluctantly, the surgeon changed the operation date to June, a few weeks after I'd return from a two-week solo hike in southern Utah.

Meanwhile, the September 11 tragedy continued to unravel me. Not always outwardly visible, the tears and despondency were as relentless as a tornado, wreaking terrible havoc on my life. The media couldn't be trusted, yet I couldn't stop watching, listening, reading about every new turn of events, every sad discovery, and the endless replays of that infamous September morning. What was I looking for? Desperate to dig some meaning out of the wreckage, I flew to New York City soon after planes were allowed in the air. Cameras slung around my neck and across my shoulders, I emerged from the subway on Vesey Street and made my way to ground zero.

I don't know what I expected. Perhaps some revelation was around the corner: I felt a kind of anticipation that was a puzzling mix of excitement and dread. The visual impact wasn't immediate. Debris in the streets, mangled pieces of steel leaning against undamaged buildings. New Yorkers went about their business as usual, but in that river of people flowing in a steady current past the heavily guarded site, there was a palpable grief. I'd come here to connect with this, to make sense of it, but now I found I didn't want to. The intensity of this experience paralyzed even my tears.

Back home, I couldn't find solace anywhere, and frankly, panic set in. My reaction began to feel disproportionate to the event. After all, so many people had suffered tragic personal losses from this, and I was merely a witness. Yet the despair I felt wouldn't go away. It became so oppressive that I began to wonder if I'd gone insane. It was now late October and I had to find peace somehow, but how? And where? One night at 11:30 p.m., I turned off the channel that was replaying newsreel footage of the smoking debris and went outside. I lay down on the soft grass and looked up at the sky as clouds drifted across the moon. Focusing only on the clouds and how their shapes changed, the first feeling of peace, as light as a feather, landed on my heart. Then, a lone plane made its way overhead through the ink blue sky, and tears came all over again. Where in the world was this sadness taking me?

The TV sat mute for a few weeks while I worked on a plan. Insanity hadn't captured me after all, but I'd been deeply wounded and I had to figure out a way to recover. Not ever having navigated territory like this before, I did the only thing I knew how to do.

I made two lists.

In one I wrote all the things about me and my life that I wanted to change. I confess it was long and contained everything from "get more sleep" to "stop being so judgmental." In the other, I wrote all of the positive traits I never wanted to lose. It was, naturally, a much shorter list, but I realized immediately that it held information about the core of who I thought I was. If I could tap those strengths, I felt certain I could find my way out of the dark labyrinth in which I was stuck.

After a long look at the "change" list, I identified what wouldn't require a lot of energy, angst, or adjustment. Things like "get more exercise," "drink more water," and "get more sleep," could be fairly easily worked into my day—I just had to be consistent.

The other things were harder to figure out. How do you stop being judgmental when you're not really sure why you're that way to begin with? So I went down the list and found something I could probably do in the course of a regular day: "be kinder to people" and "stop pushing people away." I knew this was just the tip of the iceberg and that as I worked on my list, I'd probably uncover clues to my sadness, bits of information and shreds of memories I'd buried for a reason.

This, I knew, was going to be really hard. So, as I sat there with my lists, several pages long and messily written, I decided something. To heal myself, to pull myself out of the ashes and make myself into a new and better person, I was going to give myself a year. No romantic relationships, no job changes, no major decisions—just the personal work. Solitude and introspection were about to become my best friends.

In June, I reported to the hospital for surgery. Afterward, the results were both interesting and good: I didn't have two tumors, I had four, and one of them was the size of a cantaloupe. But they were benign. The doctor held my hand when she gave me the good news, then asked me to try to sit up and walk a bit if I could. The nurses in the room held their breath as I slowly swung my legs out to the side of the bed. One of them cringed. But I stood straight up and took a few shuffling steps around the room.

"Doesn't it hurt?" one of them asked, incredulous.

"A little bit," I said, thinking to myself that compared to my riding accident this felt like a massage.

The doctor was delighted. "We're going to keep you over-night," she said, "but it's looking very likely you'll go home tomorrow. Good job!"

The next morning I woke up feeling a strange sort of anxiousness. I put my hand on my abdomen, which was distended, purple, and extremely hot. The nurse I summoned suggested we call the doctor. Doctor's orders were to get me to a CAT scan immediately. Within an hour of the scan, I was being prepped for emergency surgery.

"You've got internal bleeding," the surgeon told me as the nurses attached tubes and disconnected the IV drip. Her face concerned me: She looked exhausted, as if she hadn't slept in days, and there was a glassy sheen over her eyes. "We have to operate on you right now."

"But I've eaten, and . . ."

"We'll take care of that. We need to take you *now*."

I placed a quick call to work to leave an update, and the next thing I knew I was being whisked down the hall with a sense of urgency I didn't like. Four and a half hours later, as I was being brought out of anesthesia and still in the operating room, I heard my name and felt someone shaking my shoulder. Behind her mask, the surgeon told me I needed a blood transfusion. Groggy and disoriented, I told her to go ahead. "You didn't sign the consent," she said. "We need you to sign it." Someone put a pen in my hand and held a paper up for me to sign. A nurse had to help me. The very moment I had finished my signature, the needle was inserted into my arm and the transfusion began. Three seconds later I began to feel the deepest physical pain I've ever felt, as if the marrow in my bones was freezing solid. The moans coming out of my mouth sounded like those of a wounded animal, and then I began to convulse.

Everything and everybody stopped. I remember a moment of silence before the surgeon said, "Did you cross-type her for antibodies?"

"Yes, this is the right blood," answered a nurse. "Should we stop?"

There was a long pause before the surgeon said, "No."

"Oh my God," I heard. "We forgot to warm the blood."

My moaning turned to cries of "Help me, help me!" while my body jerked and shook on the gurney. I was freezing from the inside out. Although conscious, I could no longer see. All around me I heard a flurry of activity, but I felt something tugging at me and recognized that feeling from a long time ago, when death first tried to take me. I recognized that moment before dying, when death's hand comes to pull at you. I was leaving my body and I thought, *This is* not *how I want to die. I'm not ready yet!* I started flailing one of my arms.

"What is she doing?" someone asked.

"Hold my hand," I shouted. A warm, strong hand grabbed mine and that's what kept me alive. I squeezed as hard as I could until I felt death turn and leave, foiled for the second time.

When I left the hospital several days later, I realized I'd been given a gift, an opportunity to acknowledge that death could be around any corner and if I was going to start living the life I wanted, I had better start doing it now.

I made five more trips out to the canyons after that and still couldn't bring myself to get on a rope and rappel down into the unknown. But I was falling deeply in love with that part of the country, my visits there more and more spiritually fulfilling. I spent a lot of time on long hikes alone, thinking about how I wanted my life to go.

In 2004, I finally had the nerve to look at my quarterly mutual fund statement—the mutual fund I'd set up to invest my travel money—and my jaw literally dropped. After the financial hit it had taken post-September 11, it had rebounded with a fury. Not only had it gained everything back but had almost doubled in the last quarter. I thought about finally getting myself to Italy but decided on the Costa Rica riding vacation instead. Maybe riding new and different horses would help me get over the post-accident anxiousness I still felt when riding Brazen.

A few months later I was on a plane to Central America. Getting there was a trial from the very beginning, every omen suggesting I should cancel the trip. But I persevered, even when the originating flight was grounded on takeoff due to failed engine hydraulics. This caused missed connections, a flight into a different airport, a long and almost unbearable six-hour taxi ride on the potholed, sketchy Costa Rican roads. I'd never been so frustrated by a trip in my life and wanted to return home immediately.

There was a new vendor for the trip, a strapping, exceedingly pleasant German woman named Erica, who was an excellent rider with excellent horses. The owner of the travel company, an international one, was there to make sure that this inaugural ride went well. When she discovered I was an equine photographer, she asked if I would take some pictures for the new catalog. I had a strong vision of what I wanted to see; a rendition of the photo I'd seen all those years ago—a woman riding a horse at surf's edge—but with a bit of a twist. I explained what I thought we should do. "I love it!" the owner shouted. We had the white horse. We had the blue surf. Now we just needed a tanned, capable rider with long blond hair who would gallop the horse down the beach, trailing a green sarong behind her.

The rider I had in mind, another riding vacation customer, was unavailable. "Janice," said the travel company owner, "you're going to have to ride. I think I can manage the photos."

I was hoisted atop this difficult, unruly horse who seemed so angry he literally bit at the air. The job ahead was to gallop this white, foaming nightmare up and down the beach while the travel company owner took pictures for the catalog. The saddle stirrups were too long, I was in a bathing suit, and my bare legs chafed against wet, sandy leather. And, to get the image I'd envisioned, I had to gallop as fast as I could, with one hand holding the reins and the other hand trailing a bright green sarong behind me. All eyes were on me, I wasn't going to back out, but I kept having flashbacks to the riding accident that awful July afternoon eight years earlier.

At the point I was sitting on top of this horse, I'd been riding most of my life. But this horse's gait—a crazed combination of full-out gallop and full-up rearing with some rodeo thrown in— was nothing I'd felt before. If I could have held on to the saddle horn with both hands and been hog-tied in the saddle, I *still* would have had trouble staying put.

So our galloping was more of a canter, something I could control, something that wasn't going to pitch me to the ground if all went awry. But the pictures were lackluster, so the travel company owner kept asking me to go faster. I tried, but I was bouncing all over the place, and frankly, it was not only scary, it hurt.

Then I remembered what I'd thought about in the hospital, when I felt myself going away after the blood transfusion. Losing my life in a hospital wasn't how I wanted to die. But this, riding in the surf on a Costa Rican beach, would make a worthy exit. As I rode away from the camera to set up another shot for what felt like the hundredth time, the horse started prancing instead of pitching. It was such a lovely, collected, and animated gait, we felt perfectly connected. We were one. It felt right. And the ten-year-old girl I used to be said *"Go for it!"*

So I did. I galloped that wild thing with every ounce of resolve I had. Those first few bolting and potent strides struck my heart beatless. I couldn't breathe. We galloped down the beach as if lions were chasing us. My mouth cracked a smile so wide the sun shone right through the back of my head. Two strides into this caper and the fear that had closed so many doors in my heart was a just a dot in the distance. The ten-year-old Janice was back, triumphant. I knew I was going to fall off that horse, but I didn't care. I felt the way I hadn't felt in a long time—alive and indestructible.

At the end of the photo shoot, the travel company owner ran up to me, shouting excitedly, "I got the shot, I got the shot!" Indeed, there it was: a pale-skinned, dark-haired woman galloping a white horse through the blue surf of Costa Rica. That picture became iconic, appearing in advertisements and promotions all over the world. I remembered what I'd thought about all those years ago, when I'd looked at the advertisement for the Costa Rica ride and thought, *I want to be her*. Well, now I was.

That day in Costa Rica brought me something else, too: a resolve to battle fear, to try to open the doors it had closed in my heart, and to keep it from slamming any more of them shut. The next year, I would go to Utah and finally get into a slot canyon by rope. Although it had taken many, many steps to get to that point, I felt that was where my journey really began.

After more than a decade of traveling alone, I figured out what I wanted to pack in my metaphorical suitcase, and it's four key essentials for life's journey.

Essential number one is solitude. You cannot think deeply, in any kind of extended way, about anything until you spend alone time with yourself. An hour here or there is a start but it doesn't get you far enough. You need *days* to wrestle with the big questions we all need to be asking ourselves. Those questions are different for each of us. If you want to realize your potential, if you want to know what *really* matters to you, you need to be by yourself for a while. You need to take time to think about things deep in that place where you tell the truth.

Essential number two is introspection. Within your alone time—if you don't fill it up with e-mail, iPods, cell phones, magazines, and other fluff—you will have a chance to visit or revisit some of those things you've had trouble grasping before. Sometimes, if you're lucky and diligent, you'll figure out what might make you happy versus what you know will not. Maybe you need to figure out the next chapter in your life. Maybe, like me, you need to figure out why you are the way you are, and then map a plan to change. Introspection is not easy. It's a discipline, a sort of meditation. There is a temptation to say "I am too old to change, and I'm not that bad anyway." That's just fear talking. Nothing and no one should be satisfied with stasis. If you are brave enough to face yourself and to be brutally honest, you are ready for the next key.

Essential number three is courage. Are you brave? How do you know? Do you *want* to be courageous? You are brave if you tackle something that scares you when the option of retreat is available. The fear should be the kind that makes you feel faint, or that makes you think you're going to pee your pants, or that unravels you so much you'd rather eat a can full of worms than do the thing that's facing you. But in order to find out who you are and what you're made of, you *must* push your envelope to the very fringes of your limits. And then you must push it some more. You will be completely and utterly amazed at what happens.

Essential number four is commitment. It's not enough to carve out alone time once, or give serious thought to a problem one time, or overcome a single challenge and consider it done. I've sworn "never again" after almost every adventure trip that left physical and psychological scars. But less than 12 months later, I was back again for more. Harder, longer, with fewer ways out. As much as I've learned about what I'm capable of, I've learned what I'm not. I know my limits. It's both humbling *and* empowering. It's been the single most profound self-development strategy I've embraced, and it's all because of traveling alone.

Ultimately, though, commitment, which comes at the end of this cycle, is really about *not* settling for a life that is less than what you want for yourself. I am not referring to material wealth, which is meaningless if you are not fulfilled. I'm talking about living a life full of vigor and energy and courage, a life that inspires you and others, a life that makes you feel you are not simply biding time, waiting for the next best thing.

The chapters that follow are my own journeys of exploration into courage, solitude, introspection, and a commitment to all three. If you follow me, in your own way, down these paths, you will never go back to the life you had before. You will become fully alive. There is no better feeling, and no better gift to you and to the world.

You've been endowed with human life. Here's a way to sculpt something grand out of it.

CHAPTER TWO

COURAGE

Courageous action happens in spite of doubts and insecurities and bewilderment. It happens like the fast-forward blossoming of a flower—breathtaking and unstoppable.

HUNDREDS OF FEET of sheer cliff gaped below me. Too frightened to look, I focused on the red rope in my hands, the orange Navajo sandstone at my feet, and the impossibly blue southern Utah sky above. The tears I was determined not to shed blurred them all together as I inched backward toward the biggest and most terrifying rappel of my life. Fear literally shook my bones—so hard I thought they would break.

Three men watched. One of them laughed. Yawning at my back was the slot canyon; a fanged, cavernous maw; a tiger's mouth.

I felt as if I stepped off the edge, I'd be eaten alive.

One timid tiptoe after another led me to the stepping-off point. I couldn't bear to look down, but I did manage a glance behind me. The other side of the canyon was an enormous, sheer rock face that loomed hundreds of feet up *and* down. I collapsed to my knees. Shaking, banging my helmet-clad forehead against the rock, I whispered, "Why are you so scared, why are you so scared?"

A raven cawed from somewhere deep inside the canyon.

The men watched, but none of them helped. Desperate, I realized I had to do this thing alone. Fear turned to anger and that somehow forced my legs to get me upright and moving. Everything hinged on one final, epic step into thin air.

Do it!

I thought my heart would rip right out of my chest when I leaned backward onto the rope.

Then an odd thing happened.

When I stepped over my fear, it simply went away. Once I'd made those first tentative vertical steps, I looked down, and instead of feeling nauseated, I thought, *This is so amazing!* All I'd needed was one fleeting yet herculean moment of courage to move one foot off the ramp and into the vast emptiness of the canyon below.

Giddy, I made my way down the rock face, leaning back against the rope, placing one foot, then the other, against the bright orange sandstone. It seemed so easy, but a hundred feet later, I lost my footing as the wall receded—and this is how I went into my first free rappel. Gently and easily. There was no one to ask for direction, so I figured it out for myself. I started spinning as the canyon floor got closer, and I could see the end of the rope. It looked as though I'd just rappel right off the end and fall a couple of feet onto nice soft sand. My heart never stopped pounding, but now it was from exhilaration, not fear. The rope was about three feet too short. At the bottom, I let go and dropped to the ground, then jumped up and let out a whoop so loud that the echo returned to me four times.

I USUALLY DON'T ADMIT to hearing voices in my head, but that's exactly how I ended up in southern Utah, in a dark slot canyon, dangling from a rope. And it was all because I needed to get away. Six years into my challenging job as CEO for a Girl Scout council in North Carolina, things weren't getting any easier. The daily crises had piled up so high I could no longer see the path ahead. After a particularly grueling week, I decided I needed a vacation, to go off and do something that would completely distract me from the stresses of daily life. I thought about riding horses in Spain, but the voice inside my head kept whispering *Utah, Utah, Utah*. Why Utah? Why not Rosebud or a day at the spa or dark chocolate?

The Utah idea wasn't as random as I make it sound. I'd wanted to go there to fulfill a dream I'd had since I was 17, a dream of exploring slot canyons the way they are meant to be explored, by rope.

Slot canyons. Carved by water, wind, and time, they are beautiful, sensual, sublime sculptures of intense erosion, where ribbons of millennia are exposed before your eyes. You cannot imagine anything so weird, so strange, and so exquisite all at the same time. It's like seeing the very bones of Earth.

But it was going to require some marshaling of personal resources on my part. I'm afraid of heights, so rappelling off 200-foot cliffs into the dark recesses of Earth would require a level of courage that so far I'd not been able to muster. Many times I'd intended to explore the canyons by rope, and just as many times I'd chickened out. The closest I came to navigating a canyon was walking up a trail on the steep side of one, holding onto chains to keep from falling to my death. It scared me so thoroughly, I'd decided that an attempt at canyoneering would probably send me into cardiac arrest. Thirteen times I went to Utah to get into a canyon, and thirteen times I failed. It was my own sad little secret.

I'm not an athlete. The only "extreme" thing I'm good at is sleeping in, and that skill doesn't transfer well to canyons. I also have a rare ability to slip and fall while standing in line at the grocery store. But for some time I'd been feeling the need to do something to shake off my stasis. I remember actually saying out loud to someone, "I think I need to scare the crap out of myself." So I signed up for a three-day canyoneering school, near Zion National Park in Utah, taught by one of the most respected canyon guides in the United States. Thirteen tries had to be good for something. Maybe the 14th time would be the charm.

In my excitement about canyoneering school, I told some friends about it. Every one of them told me I was crazy and tried to talk me out of it. Like a sliver under the skin, their words began to irritate me. Then I felt a small knot of doubt tightening in my stomach. *Was* I crazy?

It had been 27 years since I first saw those pictures of slot canyons, and my 44th birthday loomed on the horizon. I realized that somewhere along the way, fear had taken over. Every accident or mishap had become a justification for doing less. I made a list of all the things I was afraid to do because I'd either been banged up by them or thought I would be: galloping a horse over fences, bungee jumping, hang gliding, surfing, and of course, rappelling into the unknown. What was next on the list, I wondered? What was the next thing I'd talk myself out of doing? I was sick and tired of fear running the show and disgusted with myself for letting it.

The school sent me a precourse kit, and I practiced my knot-tying skills every night. I was supposed to learn four knots and four hitches and know them cold. The whole knot-tying thing seemed too much like domestic work so I approached it with a distinct lack of enthusiasm. By the time I left for Utah, I could tie all the knots and hitches, but only if I had the guidebook in one hand and the rope in the other.

THREE WEEKS LATER, I was driving out of Las Vegas toward Utah as if my hair was on fire, and considering it was 117°F in the shade, spontaneous combustion was not out of the question. In the rearview mirror, the Las Vegas skyline became smaller, and the mountains before me loomed larger, but it would be three and a half more hours of driving through the desert, interrupted only by towns with names like Mesquite and Hurricane and Virgin, before I hit the spectacular entrance to Zion National Park.

The ritual of leaving Las Vegas holds so much symbolism for me—driving away from the prison of my obligated life, toward the promise of peace, beauty, and the pure truth of nature. As with any ritual of letting go, I thought about what I was leaving behind. The week before I'd been wrestling with all the problems a CEO job promises: trying to raise $200,000 to fund a program; a management team fighting with one another; a $300,000 roof that leaked. Then, 15 minutes before a big grant application was due, a customer called, threatening to sue. To cap off the week, the board chair paid an unannounced visit at 5:55 p.m. on Friday. She loved to show up at quitting time and harass me. At 7:30, we were still in my office, me stewing quietly while "Dee" (as she insisted I call her) ticked off her list of current complaints.

When I was finally behind the wheel of my car that night, all the pent-up anger, fury, and frustration spewed out of me in the form of tears. I hate to cry. It feels like such a loss of control, and it makes me even angrier than the situation that got me there in the first place.

NOW I WAS BEHIND THE WHEEL AGAIN, but thousands of miles away. With each mile I gained on Zion, I left a little bit of worry in my wake, a little bit of angst, until I made the turn onto Highway 9 and started the last leg of the drive. Most everything in my head was gone now, except for the sick feeling in my stomach over "Dee." She was a hard worry to shake. When I stopped to fuel the car, I put the top down on the rented convertible. As I approached Zion, the wind through my hair whisked away any final thoughts of her. The canyon was coming.

I KNOW THE DRIVE TO ZION WELL. There's a bend in the road and suddenly there it is, waiting to take your breath away with grand cliffs and spires and red rocks glowing in the setting sun. This time, yellow sunflowers bloomed in profusion alongside the road. Behind them, emerald green river grass grew along a creek and filled pastures that ran right up to the base of enormous orange cliffs that 175 million years ago were the highest and largest sand dunes on Earth. All those millions of years of geologic history are exposed in Zion Canyon, and as I entered the park, I felt humbled by it.

On either side of the road, the canyon walls became steeper, taller, and closer. Inside those massive cliffs were the slots, their magnificent secrets hidden from sight. To envision a slot canyon, take about a mile of the most colorful part of the Grand Canyon and press it together so it is only five feet wide where the Colorado River cuts through. Then, where this compression begins, give the river about ten huge, boulder-strewn stair steps as it makes its way down to Lake Mead. That's what a slot canyon is like: spectacularly beautiful, narrow, steep, overwhelming in grandeur, seductive yet daunting, dangerous to navigate. And every once in a while, in this slot canyon that was created just yesterday, geologically speaking, the spring rains and snowmelt fill its river with so much water that it swells and smashes through the slot's narrow twists and turns, violently altering the landscape, so that what yesterday was an angular and jagged rock face is now as smooth and rounded as a woman's shoulder. That's how fast it can happen, and it's been happening like that for millions of years.

Tomorrow I would be inside one of those secret slots. I tried not to think too much about the risks. Deep inside a slot canyon you are terribly vulnerable to the whims of nature and your own stupidity. You can end up in the news or the obituaries. Remember the infamous story about the guy who got caught in a canyon and had to cut off his arm to get free? That was Aron Ralston, and canyoneering alone is what he was doing when a boulder rolled onto his arm and trapped him. Many canyoneers have died while being overtaken by sudden and violent flash floods. The physical risk in canyoneering is, quite simply, as extreme as the beauty.

The little town of Springdale is at the western entrance to Zion National Park, and after 13 prior visits, I knew exactly where I wanted to stay and what I wanted to eat. I settled into my favorite hotel then savored dinner in front of floor-to-ceiling windows that framed a glorious rock face. Later, I swam in the heated pool overlooking another million-dollar view. I remember driving the convertible slowly through the park, top down, to watch the moonrise, and smiling into the night: I was finally here to do what I had been intending to do for almost three decades.

I slept that night the way I used to on Christmas Eve, full of excitement about what would await me in the morning. Whatever it was, I thought that I was ready.

THE FIRST RAYS OF SUN were just beginning to touch the top of the mountain peaks when I pulled into the outfitter's parking lot at 7 a.m. Soon, another student arrived. He looked to be about my age, despite the silver hair under his baseball cap and his carefully trimmed white beard. "Major" Payne was a retired Army doctor. I made a mental note that no matter how you construed his name, it didn't bode well for his bedside manner. Payne had exited his car dressed in hiking gear and ready to go. His pale blue eyes suggested a keen focus on something other than meeting me.

"Have you ever done anything like this before?" I asked as we shook hands.

"Nope," he answered, smiling. "I like to try one new thing every year, and this year it's the canyons."

Our conversation was interrupted by the sound of tires squealing, and I turned to see a small, banged-up car belching blue exhaust. It peeled into the parking lot and lurched to a stop. Out popped a young man in camo flip-flops and Bermuda shorts, so thin he looked like an upright spaghetti noodle. His flaming red hair swirled like soft-serve ice cream. He opened the hatch on his car and started tearing into a pile of debris. I walked over and asked if he was taking the course. "Big Red," a 24-year-old engineering student, gave me a perfunctory glance with narrowed eyes, then turned back to his task. He seemed desperate to find something in the mound of clothes and beer cans and garbage. Maybe he's looking for his boots, I thought, looking down at his questionable footwear. "Here it is!" he said, and triumphantly pulled out earbuds and an MP3 player from under a greasy Burger King bag. At the same time, a tall, fit, and very handsome man exited the outfitter building and walked straight toward us.

"I'm Jonathan," he said, shaking our hands. He looked at Red's MP3 player and smiled. "You won't have any time for that on this trip, I'm afraid," he said, then looked at Red's feet.

"Do you have any other footwear?" Red recommended rifling through his pile while Payne and I followed Jonathan into the building. I thought there might be more students arriving, but it was just the three of us, and we were all in the beginner class, eager to be molded by Jonathan into expert canyoneers. Jonathan, as I had come to find out via the Internet, had an impressive adventure résumé that included appearances on TV and in magazines. Despite all that and his model-worthy good looks, he seemed genuine and down to earth.

Red found his boots and joined us inside the building. Jonathan described the three-day plan. Today would be our introduction to the basics of canyoneering, otherwise known as ground school.

Tomorrow we'd tackle a different kind of slot canyon, one that was mostly wide open but had a number of typical canyoneering challenges: down climbs, plunge pools, scrambling. I didn't know what any of that meant, but Jonathan described it with such a lack of drama that it sounded doable. The third day, Jonathan said, we would test all our newly acquired skills by navigating an active canyon with waterfalls.

He smiled. "All right, let's get to it!"

Naturally, I assumed that ground school meant *on the ground*. We piled into a Land Rover and headed toward a canyon about 30 minutes outside the park boundary. On the way, Jonathan handed us some rope and asked us to demonstrate our knot-tying acumen. Payne aced the test. Red and I struggled, but at least he had an excuse: he'd received his precourse kit only a few days before. I had no reasonable explanation as to why all my knot-tying practice was for naught, so I didn't even bother trying to explain. My eyes crossed and my tongue stuck out the corner of my mouth as I tried valiantly, over and over, to tie a water knot. Payne and Red looked at each other. They tried to be discreet, but I saw their eyebrows go up. *It's just ground school,* I thought. *I'll practice tonight and be an expert water knotter by tomorrow.*

From the road our destination canyon looked like a giant, petrified mud heap in the middle of a field. Not intimidating in the least. We hiked in through twists and turns and up steep little hills until we reached a flat spot where Jonathan told us to stop. There, on top of the brown, rocky soil, we laid out our gear and began to learn the basics. First came our harnesses. Red stepped right into his and began adjustments while Payne and I either put ours on backward or upside down. When Jonathan offered to help, it seemed so simple an eight-year-old could do it. "Pull your leg straps tight," he said, "and make sure the harness sits on your hips, not at your waist." I made my adjustments, and the whole thing felt quite comfortable, until Jonathan grabbed my harness in the front and tugged on it so hard I lost my footing. "Too loose," he said. "There should be no movement front to back or side to side." I pulled on the leg straps and he yanked on the hip strap and I felt like I was being squeezed into shorts that were three sizes too small. It turned out that would be the least of my worries.

Next came an explanation of locking carabiners, the protocol of the safety tether. Jonathan presented each piece of gear with a demonstration; we watched, handled, then clipped whatever it was onto our harness rings.

Jonathan said something I didn't like: He told us he would be 100 percent there for us today, less so tomorrow, and by day three he said he'd be "a liability." This could mean only one thing: I really had to listen and pay attention. No daydreaming or cloud busting or thinking about the fabulous meal I planned to eat that night.

Jonathan also informed us that we'd do most of our own problem solving. It began almost immediately, when he asked us to choose an anchor—something secure to tie the rope around—and then once we had, we had to explain the logic behind our choice. The choice of an anchor is a pretty big deal because it's what keeps you from falling to your death. In a well-traveled canyon there are usually bolts to use as anchors, and as long as they've been properly inserted into the rock, bolts are the way to go. But Jonathan wanted to make sure that we could identify an anchor, in case bolts were not an option. If the anchor is a tree, you tie a "sling" around it: a long piece of webbing about the size and width of riding reins, with one or two sliding metal rings on it. Once the sling is tied around the anchor, the rappelling rope goes through the rings. Where you position the knot and the angle at which you set your rope are both very important choices, Jonathan told us. We tied the sling to a little pine tree, and Jonathan made some adjustments. If you position the rope here—he demonstrated, pulling the sling high up the tree—"You're stressing the root system more than if you tie the sling as close to the roots as you can." He moved it down. Payne and Red nodded. *God,* I thought, *I hope I can remember all this.* I seemed to be the only one who wasn't eating up this information like candy.

I was beginning to think I was in over my head. We hadn't even gotten to the hard part yet, and I wasn't fully absorbing the critical information flowing like a river out of Jonathan's mouth. Some important piece of instruction would float right by on his current of words, and then it was gone, never to be retrieved. *This isn't what I thought I was getting into. Can I go home now?*

Part of our orientation included how to thread our rappelling device (a nasty-looking piece of equipment that goes by the name Pirana) with single and double ropes, how to determine which set-ups would allow us to go faster or slower, and what to do if you don't have enough rope.

I was impressed by Jonathan's knowledge. And, as the instructions went on, Jonathan's calm and gentle way of teaching began to calm me down. I started to feel like maybe, just maybe, everything was going to be OK. I asked so many questions that Payne and Red both crossed their arms and started tapping their feet. I heard the occasional exasperated sigh. I didn't care. There was no telling what was around the next corner, but while I had Jonathan within arm's length, I was going to try to extract every bit of information I could.

With the basics covered, we hiked and scrambled up a few steep little slopes, and I still didn't have the sense that we had gained much elevation. Then we came to the site of our first rappel and my hands started to shake. Gray boulders as big as houses flanked the trail, which five feet ahead of us narrowed to just a few feet wide, then dropped into blackness. I stayed far away from the edge, but Red walked right over there to the ramp—the stepping-off point—and inspected the slot. My heart clunked around in my chest.

I watched Red get "on rope" and begin his rappel. It didn't take long for his whole body to disappear from view into the dark slot below. Halfway down he let out a whoop and I heard it echo off the canyon walls. I looked at the rope setup and suddenly nothing made sense. What if the bolts come out of the wall? What if the rope breaks? What if I pee my pants?

Payne went next. He looked completely in control of himself, except when it came time for him to step off and I noticed one of his legs shaking. *Good,* I thought, *at least I'm not the only one.* While Payne descended, huffing and puffing, I stood perfectly still, hoping that I might disappear.

Silence for a long time, then the echo of Payne shouting, "Off rope!"

Jonathan smiled at me. "Your turn, Janice."

I looked at the entrance to the slot—a dark, round hole only a little larger than my body. Folds of gray rock surrounded it.

It looked like a throat.

I was about to be swallowed by the canyon.

What I learned in that moment was that there are two kinds of fear—the kind that keeps you from stepping off the edge of a cliff when you shouldn't and the kind that keeps you from stepping off the edge of a cliff when you should. As I stood on the precipice of my first rappel, I tried to recognize the difference. But at that moment, fear was fear, with all of its demons and distractions. I wasn't afraid of falling. I wasn't afraid of dying. I was just afraid. *OK,* I said to myself, *you're afraid. Now get it together and step off the edge.*

In a brief moment of clarity I understood that this moment could never be duplicated in my life. Never again would I take my first intentional step off a cliff. As I took the biggest step of my life, I let the rope hold me, and it did. Down I went, shaky foot by shaky foot, a burning smell reminding me of how much friction the rope was having to endure as it slid through the Pirana. The harness hurt my hip bones and the straps cut into my legs, but I barely noticed. The canyon floor was getting closer. Gravity was working with me. I was going to make it! I arrived at the end of my rope with a smile on my face, even though my heart beat so crazily it sounded like a bongo festival.

Here I was, finally, 50 feet inside a slot. As my eyes adjusted to the dim light, I looked all around. It was more breathtaking than I'd dreamed it would be. Surrounding me, columns of orange-pink Navajo sandstone twisted upward like giant human torsos in an unchoreographed dance. It was impossibly beautiful, as if the huge curves and sweeps of rock had been deliberately sculpted not by water and wind but by something mysterious and with a purpose.

Jonathan zipped down the rope and asked for our feedback. "Awesome," said Red. "Great fun," Payne added. Jonathan looked at me. I wasn't willing to let my game face down this early on, so I pretended to be unmoved. "I don't know," I said, "ask me at the end of the day." He told me my posture needed work. "Lean back into the rope," he said, "Try bouncing off the walls. Have *fun*, Janice!"

Off we hiked on even ground to the next rappel, but before reaching it, we first had to complete a series of down climbs, a tricky bit of maneuvering Jonathan had mentioned early in the morning. Here, the floor of the canyon where we stood went from flat to what looked like a chute, and it ended at the edge of a dark crack. Jonathan asked for suggestions on how to maneuver this part. It was too steep to walk on but not really steep enough to set a rope. Red offered to scoot down on his butt.

"How will you get back up if that's a 30-foot drop?" Jonathan asked.

"Let me throw a rock," I offered, but Jonathan was quick to tell us that canyoneers never throw rocks over an edge. Someone might be coming up-canyon, he explained.

"One of you needs to go down on rope and check out the crack," Jonathan told us, "so let's find an anchor." I twirled around, searching, but the canyon walls were as smooth as glass.

"Are we going to do a meat anchor?" Red asked, and Jonathan nodded. I had momentary visions of anchoring the rope to a giant rump roast, but it turned out that the "meat" was us: Payne, Jonathan, and I tied a rope around our bodies and Red zipped down the smooth chute into the inscrutable crack. He disappeared for a moment then pulled his way back up. "It's about ten feet," he reported, "but really narrow. You guys come down and you can use me as a step."

This was my first down climb and it felt totally out of control, like scooting down a steep patch of ice on my butt. My feet slid on the sand as I inched my way toward that crazy swirling flame of hair sticking out of the holes in the helmet on the top of Red's head. I could see only the top of Red's body and calculated the potential damage I would do if I just let go and slid smack into him.

"Come on," he said, "I'm here." I slid and shimmied to the edge of the crack and looked down. The canyon turned right at a 90-degree angle and began to bulge inward. Below Red there was one flat spot, then the canyon narrowed to no more than two feet wide. He helped me get from the ledge to the floor, but it was still awkward and I slipped when I stepped on his kneecap.

While Red waited for Payne to make his way down, I surveyed what lay ahead. The canyon walls were now sheer cliffs pressing in on both sides of us. The color of the rock had changed from orange-pink to an ominous dark brown. In front of me were a series of "steps"—a flat spot, then a six-foot drop, another flat spot, then an eight-foot drop. Up ahead, there were places where the canyon narrowed to a crack only large enough for a child's arm to squeeze through. And it was chilly in there, even though the sun blazed above us in the faraway sky.

Once Red, Payne, and I were all standing on the floor, looking with confusion at what lay in front of us, Jonathan's voice drifted down from overhead. He was about four feet above us, his long legs *straddling* the canyon walls directly overhead. Jonathan's feet and hands pressed against the rock, as if he were trying to push the canyon apart. Red was impressed and I was too, but also bewildered. How did he get up there?

"There are a couple of ways to get down this slot," Jonathan said, retracing our steps back to where we'd come down the chute, then expertly hopping on a few rocks to position himself for straddling the wall. "You can down-climb or you can do what I'm doing."

"*Cool!*" Red shouted, and straddled the walls in a perfect imitation of Jonathan. Since I was first in line, I walked over to the first drop. The canyon floor was just six feet below, but the canyon walls squeezed both my shoulders. I tried to turn around, to navigate the drop backward, but my backpack jammed me in there. "Can I take this off?" I asked Jonathan.

"Is there any way for you to get down there with it on?" he answered. I had a hard time finding footholds because I couldn't see what I was doing, so I hugged the rock in front of me, lowered myself as far as I could down the six-foot drop, then let go.

The canyon floor was littered with rocks and small boulders and I twisted my ankle a little. *Don't get hurt this early on in the game!* I chided myself. Payne handed down my backpack and his, and his descent was easier because I could tell him where to place his feet. At the next drop, where the canyon pressed even closer, we had no choice but to give up solid ground. Trying to replicate the "wall walking" that Jonathan had just shown us, I placed one hand and one foot on each side of the canyon and pressed. I found I could actually walk like this along the canyon walls, as long as they didn't get too wide. This part of the challenge, more than any other, was hugely threatening to me. At least when you're "on rope," I now realized, you're safe. You're supported. When you're down-climbing or scrambling, you're extremely vulnerable to falls. I didn't like it one bit. With awe and more than a little envy, I watched as Jonathan perfectly maneuvered the nuances of the canyon with all the skill and dexterity of a mountain goat.

At the approach to the second rappel, the canyon opened up a little and the rock walls went from slabs of chocolate back to the sensuous, undulating columns of the entrance. The drop to the canyon floor was steep and long. I remember thinking, how did we get from ground school to *this*? Red went first, I went second. At the very end, trying to go right when the rope wanted to go left, I lost my footing and crashed into the rock wall. Thus came my first experience with zooming from zero to fifty in two seconds flat. I still don't understand how you can be at a dead stop, with no movement whatsoever, then simply lift a foot and be instantaneously careening out of control. The more you fight gravity, the faster you go in the opposite direction. It was a lesson that would take me several scrapes and some deep, painful bruises to learn. My souvenir from this incident was a bunch of scraped knuckles and a wrecked hand that I would still have to rely on over the next two days.

On the canyon floor, sunshine sliced through a crack in the wall no wider than 12 inches. I'd seen this crack on the outside of the canyon during our hike in. I knew it was the way out because of the footprints in the sand. Footprints leading away, not entering. *So*, I thought, *you made it through day one. What a trouper.* My heart finally began to beat in a normal rhythm.

"OK, everyone," announced Jonathan, "let's have a little lunch and then climb the rope."

Climb the rope. Three little words. So innocent, so simple. So damned impossible. Jonathan gave us each a pair of ascenders;

lobster-like claws that you attach to the rope. The ascenders have tiny little teeth that grip the rope as soon as you put weight on them. The left ascender has a rope stirrup you use to leverage your body and create slack so you can slide your right ascender up the rope. It goes like this: with your right hand, slide the ascender as high as you comfortably can, then lean back into your harness to take the weight off your left ascender and the attached stirrup. That way you can slide your left ascender up to and under the right one. At that point, you stand up in the foot stirrup and this allows you to slide your right ascender farther up the rope. Left, right, left, right. It's all technique and if you don't get the hang of it right away, you try to muscle your way up, which simply doesn't work. I struggled, lurched, and thrashed. I even made up some new words. Jonathan called out suggestions. The last thing he said finally turned the lightbulb on.

"Janice, sit down in the harness when you're sliding the left ascender."

"Why didn't you just tell me that in the first place?" I yelled down.

"I did," he answered gently, "but I guess I needed to say it in a different way."

I was too out of breath to respond. In any event, I like Jonathan and—just in case he reads this—I don't ever want him to know what I was thinking about him in those moments.

I was already planning what I wanted for dinner that night and which ice-cold beverage I would indulge in first when we were finally delivered from this travail. But a night off was not to be. Jonathan informed us that we had "homework." Our assignment, which we would be tested on tomorrow, was to create a

"You aren't going to let us fall, are you?" I asked.

"No, I won't let you fall, but at this point you know enough that that shouldn't even be a possibility." *Oh, Jonathan,* I thought, *you don't know me very well. I can't even keep my shoelaces tied!*

He went on to explain that before we got on rope, we'd have a "fairly steep" two-mile hike to our destination. In Jonathan-speak, "fairly steep" means cardiac arrest. There was no trail. Not really. Just the suggestion of one through thick brush, with hairpin turn after hairpin turn, and a sharp drop on one side. Jonathan was right about one thing. It was steep. The hike would have been hard under normal circumstances, but I was carrying 35 pounds of gear on my back. Many times I had to grab at the trail with my hands. Sweat and sunscreen streaked my face and stung my eyes, ears, and nostrils. I staggered from the sheer effort and by the end of the hike I was practically doubled over from the weight of my back-pack. *This is how they get you over any remaining fear,* I thought. *They practically kill you so that rappelling, by comparison, seems like a ride at Disneyland.*

I was so glad when the damned hike was over that I couldn't wait to get on rope. But first, Jonathan asked us to choose our anchor and set up our retrievable sling. Big Red and I looked at each other.

"Go ahead," Red growled, but Jonathan intervened. "Let's do a test run on both," he suggested.

We chose our anchor—a sturdy-looking pine tree—and set up our contraptions. Mine released immediately and Jonathan nodded his approval. Red's jammed. He tried it again, and it came free but immediately caught on some rocks.

"You're going to have to pull this sling 120 feet through that"—Jonathan jerked his head in the direction of the canyon— "so be absolutely sure about your choice." We all looked down the drop at our first rappel. It was full of logjams and small trees both live and dead. I wondered, frankly, if we'd even be able to get our bodies through the tangle of debris. Nobody said anything.

"I think we need to go with simple," I said finally. "I'm worried about those carabiners getting caught on something."

Red agreed, then Jonathan suggested we try to come up with another design. "That ship has sailed, Jonathan," I said. "I don't think there's going to be any useful inventing today."

So Jonathan showed us the design choice of 99.9 percent of the canyoneering student body. It could not have been easier or simpler, and it made perfect sense. We all agreed that was the retrievable sling we would use. "This is the last time I'm going to help today," he warned. "Except for feedback, you're pretty much on your own."

We prepared the sling, attached the pull cord, then threw it into the canyon below. The thin, yellow rope sailed through the air and down, down, down onto a soft, sandy ledge. I set up a double rope, then threw the rope bags, listening for the thud when they hit ground. There would be times, Jonathan said, when we would throw the rope bag and not hear it land. Or we'd hear it land too soon. In those cases, he explained, we might have to pull the rope back up and throw it again. But this morning, that was not necessary. All throws were home runs.

Payne went first. There were so many ledges, changes in direction, and natural obstacles that navigating was a combination of scrambling and rappelling both. It took Payne some time to get down, but I eventually heard him yell "Off rope!" His voice didn't echo, so I knew that the canyon must open up down there. I quickly threaded the rope through the Pirana and off I went.

My hand was swollen and stiff from crashing into the wall the day before, and it was hard to grip the rope. I looked down at one point and saw Payne, just a dot on the wide and open canyon floor, looking up. I descended slowly, picking my way around sharp, dead tree branches lodged in the canyon crags. In one place, I needed to move about two feet to the right to navigate around a thorny bush, but I made the critical mistake, once again, of trying to fight gravity. As soon as I did, I swung hard in the opposite direction, landing on my backside in a tree growing out of a ledge. I decided at that moment, with my pride hurt and thorns in my sensitive areas, that this was *not* going to happen again.

At the bottom Payne and I high-fived each other while we waited for Red and Jonathan. Once they were safely down and off rope, Payne and Red began pulling the rappelling ropes and stuffing them in the bags. Jonathan told me to retrieve the sling.

"Be very, very careful," he said. "Gentle is the way to go on this one."

So I pulled delicately on the cord, and I could actually see it slithering along like a long, yellow worm through the debris. It disappeared for a while, but I was still taking up slack. And then it jammed. I tried to release it the way you would release a snagged fishing line, to no avail.

"Gentle," Jonathan reminded me, then took the pull cord, jiggled it ever so slightly, and the contraption came free.

The first rappel of the day had been a success for everyone. We'd made the right decisions, roped ourselves properly from start to finish, and just generally did a good job. But I had a vague sense of unease and I didn't know why. Even after the next two easy rappels I felt it. We hiked along the sandy wash to the next rappel site, where Jonathan suggested we try my retrievable sling idea. It was an easy rappel, maybe only 50 feet, and there were two routes—one led to a sandy bottom and the other to water of unknown depth. Payne and I opted for terra firma, but Red wanted the water. When he hit the end of the rappel, he sunk up to his chest in sucking, stinking mud. Whereas I would have been pissed, Red laughed it off, but Jonathan chided him for getting our ropes dirty.

"Those ropes," he reminded us, "are your lifelines. Don't abuse the ropes."

We found a scenic spot and sat down in the sun for a little sustenance and regrouping. I was pleased that I wasn't having any major problems at all, yet that odd feeling of doom was still blooming in the pit of my stomach.

We hiked a little while to a corner and there it was: an enormous, savage rock face that scared all of us. I didn't see how it was even possible to set up for this rappel. The ramp was so steep you'd have to be on rope before you could even conduct your preparations. From the looks of the sheer wall facing us on the other side of the canyon, this rappel was going to be long and vertical, and the bottom of it might possibly be somewhere in China.

"The guidebook would tell you that this is a 200-foot rappel. You have three ropes totaling 400 feet, so you have some problem solving to do," Jonathan announced. *OK,* I thought, *we won't end up in China, maybe just in Arizona somewhere.*

Jonathan sat down on the rocks and pulled an apple out of his pocket. As he bit into it and started chewing, the rest of us just looked at each other.

"Aren't you coming?" I asked.

"No," he answered, "I'll be right here. Off you go."

That prickly feeling of doom that had been blooming in my stomach was now a full-grown cactus. We trudged toward the approach to the rappel but first had to scramble up a 15-foot vertical rock face. Red went first. There were plenty of hand- and footholds for the first five feet; the last ten were as smooth as glass. I don't remember how he managed to get up there on his own, but I went next, with Payne pushing against my butt and Red yanking me by my right arm straight up and onto a small ledge. It was the only flat spot before the canyon fell away to nothingness, like sitting on the window ledge of a skyscraper. I couldn't bear to look, so I focused on helping Payne up and over. When all three of us were situated on the ledge, which offered just enough room to sit and arrange gear, Red spotted a webbing tied around a small pine tree. He sidled over to it and attached his safety tether.

"Look," he shouted, "here's our anchor!"

From back down the path I heard Jonathan call, "Are you sure you want to use that for your anchor? Who knows how long it's been there?"

During ground school, Jonathan had warned us not to take anything for granted. A webbing that might look perfectly suitable might be dry-rotted or frayed, or the rope rings might have too much wear. Red gave the webbing a cursory inspection. "It's fine," he pronounced. Normally, I wouldn't have taken his word for it—Red was turning out to be a bit of a maverick—but there was no way I was moving from my perceived safety zone. I didn't know how I was ever going to manage to get on rope, but I chose to focus on the moment, and that moment, with my butt firmly planted on the Navajo sandstone, was the only one that mattered.

Although I had gotten to the point where I didn't trust Red's judgment, I was grateful for his apparent fearlessness. Once he snapped his safety tether onto the anchor webbing, he inched his way down the ramp so he could take a look at the drop.

"*Heeee-yaaaaawwww,*" he hollered and shook his head. "That's *steep!*"

We decided how we'd use our three ropes, then Red offered to tie them. Red was not the best with knots. He was too impatient, and his knots always looked haphazard. I had become the unofficial "knot checker" (ironic, considering my near incapacity with them at the beginning), and this time was no exception. I scooted over on my butt to check them. Sure enough, they needed retying. I still hadn't looked down. I focused only on the immediate task at hand and refused to accept the inevitability of what was to come.

It's customary to get everyone's approval on the knots before the first rappel. Red and Payne gave nods, and with that, Red threw the ropes. The silence—long and intense—was finally broken by the slap of the ropes hitting the side of the canyon, not the usual thud when they hit bottom. That meant only one thing. They were too short. We'd have to rappel off the end of the unknotted rope and jump whatever distance remained.

I have a vague, sort of smeared memory of us talking about this, but it was so beyond my ability to comprehend what was about to happen that everything became surreal, like a cartoon, only not funny. I think I was shutting down. Adrenaline was narrowing my vision. Colors were becoming more vivid. Words seemed incomprehensible. Jonathan wasn't there to consult or support our decisions, we were about to face something completely new, and I didn't have it in me to be this competent or brave or fearless or stupid.

Now that the ropes were thrown and we were committed, I sat back down and waited. Payne adjusted some of his gear. Red kicked at the rock with his toe. No one wanted to go until Jonathan finally called out, his voice sounding farther and farther away.

"Who hasn't gone first?"

I felt their eyes upon me, but I looked up at the clouds and attempted a nonchalant whistle. I sputtered instead. One deep breath, then I called back to Jonathan, "I'm having a fair bit of anxiety over here."

"Sometimes," he answered calmly, "that's the best time to step up."

I waited awhile, then yelled back, hoping to buy time, "Explain to me why."

When he didn't answer, I knew there was no point in arguing or trying to negotiate. It was hopeless, and I faced the fact that I was going to have to go first. And no one, I noticed, was offering to take my place.

I gulped another deep breath, clipped my safety tether into the anchor, and got on rope. *It's just like every other rappel, Janice, it'll be OK.* I moved backward toward the ramp with the tiniest steps ever taken in the history of rappelling. With each millimeter, I felt tears coming closer and I was horrified. *You will not cry in front of these men!* I told myself, but the truth is, I was starting to unravel. Everything inside of me was coming apart.

Even in that moment, when adrenaline should have made cognition difficult, I recognized the danger of what was happening inside me. Something critical was breaking away. It was as if every ounce of my courage and tenacity had been placed in a glass, then dropped to shatter on the ground below. Inside, I felt it break and the shards of the person I thought I was flew off in every direction. Suddenly, I had nothing. I was no one. And I was stuck.

From somewhere far away I heard Big Red taunting me, saying something about the knots giving way, then Jonathan gently admonishing him. It was just wisps of sound, nothing concrete, but enough to give me something to grab onto mentally. I pulled myself out of the empty place I was in and got back to business. I *willed* myself to get right to the edge and then collapsed. *Where was this fear coming from*, I wondered, *and why was it about to devour me?*

How did I step off the edge in my terror, a terror so explosive it shattered my emotions against the canyon floor? I did it with one thought: Trust. Trust the people you're with. Trust the process. Trust that you are strong enough to do this. Trust that there are worse places to die than in this magnificent canyon.

I wasn't surprised that Red was behaving like a jackass, but I couldn't understand why Payne, a former doctor, wasn't giving me any encouragement. I looked at him one last time before I stepped off into nothing, and then I knew why. In his eyes, I could see he was just as frightened as I was.

"Here I go," I whispered, and leaned back into the rope. I looked straight up at the azure sky and took my right foot off the ramp. I poked around blindly until the face of the canyon made contact with my foot. Smiling, I looked up at Payne. I braced that one foot and lowered the other. There was the canyon wall, right where it was supposed to be.

"It's OK," I said to Payne, laughing.

"It is?" he asked. *"Really?"*

"Really," I said, still smiling, and dropped from his sight. With the men out of view, I paused for a moment to get oriented. The rock wall glowed orange and red; my feet looked so tiny pressed against it. Did I dare look down? *You're here,* I thought, *you need to experience everything.* First, I closed my eyes to take stock: my heart wasn't pounding from fear but from exhilaration, the newness of everything, the elation of having found the courage to step off the edge. When I looked down at the sandy canyon floor littered with sticks and small rocks, I felt my harness hold me safely above it. Leaning hard against the rope, I pushed away from the rock, trying to bounce off the walls as Jonathan had suggested yesterday. But then the wall began to recede, my body began to spin, and the rest of the ride was a twirling free rappel. I knew the rope was too short, so I just rappelled off the end of it and dropped to the sandy canyon floor. *I did it!* No more holding back for me. Jumping up, I whooped at the top of my lungs, listening as the echo kept returning, cheers for a job finally done.

I'D BEEN COUNTING our rappels and knew that we were more than halfway through. *Surely,* I thought, *that last mother had to be the worst.* I didn't dare ask Jonathan, though. I was afraid that any question or statement might commit me to something I didn't want to do. So I did something I have very little practice with—I kept my mouth shut.

We hiked for a while along the sandy wash until we came to our next rappel, a short drop into a deep pool. Jonathan took an inordinate amount of time to inspect it, his brow furrowed the whole time. "Take a look at this, you guys, and tell me what you think." I didn't want to point out to Jonathan that since we hadn't navigated any water obstacles yet, how the hell would we be able to render an opinion? Nevertheless, I pronounced that it looked doable. Payne and Red both agreed. Amazingly, Jonathan didn't ask us to explain ourselves. Instead, he told us there had been some flash flooding in the last month, and all of the anchors looked potentially unstable. "I'm sure it would be fine," he said, "but I think we'll hike around it instead."

Hike around it? *Hike around it?* What was he talking about? There was nowhere to hike. Vertical canyon skirted the 20-foot drop into boulder-strewn black water. I could see a flat spot on the other side but no way to get to it that didn't involve risking injury. It would be like trying to traverse the center of a billboard with only your hands and feet.

Jonathan went first. He made one, two, three Spiderman-clinging-to-the-wall vertical steps and then a jump. I looked at the wall, and I looked at the drop, and it didn't seem possible for me to do this thing. Here was where my reputation for falling would be solidified, for the last time in my life. Payne went next, then Red.

"I'm not doing that," I declared, and sat down in the sand. "No way. You guys go. Send a helicopter. I'll be OK." Jonathan chuckled, but his amusement soon turned to frustration when I wouldn't budge.

"It's easy," Red said, "look." Red came back the way he'd gone then did it again. Zip, zip, just like that. But they were taller, longer-armed, and more muscular than I. This whole undertaking seemed like child's play to the three of them.

"Easy for you because you don't care if you die or not, Carrot Top." *Good grief!* What were these mean things coming out of my mouth? Red and Jonathan said something to each other that I couldn't hear, then both made their way back. They jumped down into the sand and walked toward me. Suspicious and on high alert, I stood up and planted both feet far apart, hands on hips. The cop stance.

"I mean it," I shouted at them. *"No!"*

"Bitch," Red muttered. I knew then that I was at the end of my rope. That last big rappel had used me up. I had no poise, no game face, no special reserve. All I had left was the ability to be an asshole.

Jonathan's soothing voice wasn't working, and I told him so. "What are you going to do, drag me across?" I taunted. "Listen to me. I'm *NOT DOING THAT!*"

Jonathan used his every charm to try to convince me. I was still holding onto plan B, helicopter evacuation, when I suddenly despaired. It would be nearly impossible for an aircraft to get in or near there. So, with my spirit even more deflated, I gave in. I'd have to get out of here eventually, and this seemed the only way. Where was the courage I'd just summoned on the cliff? Why was it hiding from me?

Jonathan went first. "Put your foot here," he showed me, "and look, here's a nice jug handle to grab onto." Red was my backup, but I wasn't entirely convinced he wouldn't intentionally knock one of my feet out from under me so he could be done with my nonsense. For the few steps it took to get from one side to the other, epithets flew out of my mouth like Chinese ribbons, twisting and dancing in the canyon air. When stressed, my swearing takes on an eloquence and creativity I can't replicate at any other time.

"Wow," Jonathan said, when we got to the other side, "I don't think I've ever heard anything like that before."

"What can I say, it's a gift," I answered, breathless and thoroughly pissed off. I felt not only like an asshole but a fool and a drama queen. There was going to be no recovering from this little tantrum. They'd be making up secret nicknames for me for sure.

The three of them busied themselves with something while I sat under a tree and adjusted my attitude. Finally, Jonathan announced it was time to practice "lowering" and he needed a volunteer. "I'll do it," I said, without hesitation. I figured this was one small step on the road to redemption.

Being lowered is not as great as it sounds. While it's true that you don't have to do any work, it's also a fact that you don't have any control over anything. You have to pretend that you're dead or injured and just lie there like a sack of potatoes. Jonathan assigned Red to the task of lowering me down to the next ledge, into water. It's quite possible that at this point Red would have liked to kick me over the edge and get it over with, but with Jonathan watching, he lowered me slowly, until I disappeared over the edge. Then suddenly I dropped faster and a little chaotically. "Oops, sorry!" I heard Red call, and could also hear the smile on his face. I splashed down into the knee-deep water and untied the knot Red had used to lower me. To continue my descent, I reattached the rope through the Pirana. Down two more ledges, following the path of a trickling waterfall, I wasn't sure if this counted as one rappel or two, but I knew we were coming to the end of our adventure for the day. I sighed. *The worst is over,* I thought.

We walked for a little while until we came to a drop that narrowed down to a plunge pool. Remnants of flash flooding and heavy rains, plunge pools can either be shallow or very, very deep, and because they rarely reflect the sun, they are bone-chillingly cold. There was no way to tell how deep it was just by looking at it, so I tossed a pebble.

Bloooooooooop.

I sighed. We were going to have to do a little swimming. At this point, I knew it was useless to ask Jonathan what to do, so I started pulling rope from my bag. Meanwhile, Red scrambled down the drop with hands and feet bracing against the canyon walls on either side. *You just go on with your big bad selves,* I thought. *I'm doing it my way.*

I was the only one who used a rope and I didn't care. Once all of us were down, we stood just above the plunge pool. There was no discussing who was going first. The canyon that had before been wide and open was now so narrow it was impossible to change the order of the lineup. "Here goes," said Red, and he half-waded, half-dove into the dark water. And then he screamed, a high-pitched, girly scream full of surprise and torment.

"Sheeeee-ittttt," he gasped as he flailed on his back away from us toward dry ground. Payne went in next, tentatively putting a leg in the water.

"Oh my God," he muttered, then dove in. When his torso hit the water, he screamed too, kicking and paddling as fast as he could. I knew Jonathan was around somewhere, but I couldn't see him, and anyway, it didn't matter. Here was another step I could take on the road to redemption. I would get in that frigid water and not make a sound.

I turned my back to the others so I could just fall backward into the water and start stroking right away. I hesitated only a moment, to make *sure* I was ready to be silent. And then I dropped.

The water overtook every part of me, filling up the inside of my clothes, and I was momentarily stunned. It was so viciously cold it felt like fire. The scream inside me hurt my ears, but I didn't make a sound. No Chinese ribbons flew from my mouth. I acted as though I did this kind of thing every day, and when I got to the other side, I heard Red say, "I don't think my balls will ever descend again."

I, on the other hand, was sure they'd pop out just in time to create more trouble for us.

"Where's Jonathan?" I asked, trying to sound nonchalant but shivering so hard my teeth rattled. I looked back at the plunge pool. No Jonathan. I looked up-canyon as far as I could. No sign of him. Then I heard a crack, and he burst out of a small trail high above and next to the plunge pool. One short down climb later he joined us, dry as a bone.

"You bastard," I said.

"Did any of you look for an alternative route?" he asked, smiling.

We got a mini-lecture then about the dangers of cotton clothing.

"None of you are wearing cotton," he said, "but if you were, and you had to swim that plunge pool early in the canyon, you'd be a candidate for hypothermia. Remember," he said, "no cotton. Synthetics only. This is going to be especially important tomorrow."

Cotton or no, we were all shivering, and Jonathan pulled from his pack three dry fleece sweaters and told us to change out of our wet ones. Nothing had ever felt so luxurious and warm and dear. I hugged myself and rubbed my arms. Soon I was toasty again.

"I think we'll leave it at that for today," Jonathan announced. "You all did well. You're ready for tomorrow."

Our hike out was flat, following the wash. Snakes, chipmunks, lizards, and giant bugs shared the trail with us. As we got closer to civilization, a young boy jumped out of the bushes and I nearly knocked him over. He was maybe six or seven years old, towheaded, blue-eyed, wearing white pants and shirt, but barefoot and filthy. Dried snot and dirt looked like it had been permanently mashed into his face. Another boy, identical, emerged from the bushes, then another. Jonathan et al didn't see any of this and kept walking.

"Hello," I said to the little boys, smiling. But there were six boys now, then seven, then nine, standing there looking at me with a mix of curiosity, suspicion, and disgust. I admit the whole thing seemed beyond creepy. Jonathan, Payne, and Big Red were out of sight, and I started back on the trail, glancing over my shoulder now and then to make sure the little guys' eyes weren't glowing some radioactive green. Around another corner I almost bumped into a woman. She wore a white bonnet and an old, prairie-style dress, also white. She had a basketful of blackberries curled under the crook of one arm. She and her herd of boys were picking berries. I remembered suddenly that the infamous Colorado City polygamist cult was less than a mile down the road. I stopped to say hello. She refused to answer, and I refused to move.

"Are those your boys?" I asked. We stared at each other for what felt like a very long time. The bushes behind me rustled. Another woman, a twin to the first one, stood motionless, staring at me. The tiny hairs on the back of my neck stood on end. I took one slow, full look around then hoofed it down the trail. *You idiot,* I thought, *spooked by two women and a bunch of little boys. What a wimp.* But something had felt really wrong. I asked Jonathan about it when I caught up to them at the truck.

"They don't trust outsiders," was all he would say.

I was so grateful to pull off my canyoneering boots and my wetsuit booties and slip my shriveled feet into a pair of pink flip-flops. Such a glib color, a complete contrast to what we'd just endured. On the drive back I talked about Oscar's Cafe and how the burgers there were to die for—as big as your head and filled with two tablespoons of chopped garlic along with other condiments that made me salivate just talking about them. We agreed that's where we would eat and invited Jonathan to join us.

"I'd be happy to," he said. "Besides, we need to go over your homework assignment."

I don't know who groaned louder, me or the men.

"Tomorrow," he said, "we'll be encountering a lot of water. You can choose between a dry suit or a wet suit," he said, explaining the pros and cons. Payne and I chose the dry suits; Red went with the wet suit. Half a wet suit. His testicles had descended after all.

At dinner we talked about our day. Jonathan gave each of us an opportunity to say what was on our minds. I told him that I would rather do ten times the first day's ascending than ever, *ever* have to scramble one of those steep edges again.

"Really?" He smiled.

"Really," I answered, taking a big bite of an Oscar's Murder Burger. I chewed gleefully, but deep down I knew I'd probably just laid down some sort of canyoneering gauntlet. Jonathan assigned our homework: Learn the Munter hitch and be able to do it in our sleep.

"That's it?" I asked.

"That's it," he answered.

Piece of cake, I thought.

Later, we met at Payne's campsite to do our homework. The Munter hitch (named for Swiss mountaineer Werner Munter) seemed really simple—a basic twist of the rope you use instead of your rappelling device. With the guidebook in one hand and our ropes in the other, we tied our Munter hitches and inspected one another's work. When we all agreed we were ready for tomorrow, I went back to my hotel room and iced my hand, still aching from the day one debacle. I also spent some time admiring the deep purple and green bruises that were forming on my lower arms and legs. I hoped they'd hang on long enough for me to display them proudly when I got home.

In the hotel hot tub, I let the heat of the water lull me out of my pain. What happened to me on the big, scary rappel and how could I unhinge so completely? Everything I thought I knew about myself had disintegrated into something I didn't recognize. It was, in retrospect, more frightening to remember that feeling of collapse than to relive the rappel itself. To shatter so quickly, so thoroughly, was shocking. Maybe, I thought, everything has to fall apart before something new can happen. But in that moment, when my sense of self had been reduced to rubble, I felt a desperation I'd never experienced. And it wasn't about the canyon. It was about suddenly not knowing who I was. It was about realizing that in the clinch, when it really mattered, I didn't know if I could pull myself together or not. I was *enormously* grateful that somewhere inside of me, I was able to find just one thing to hang onto. Evidently, that's all I needed. Would I be able to summon it again when the situation demanded? I wasn't sure.

Back in my room, I practiced the Munter hitch until I could barely keep my eyes open. I stood up to stash the rope and carabiner in my pack, then suddenly decided I'd had enough. Enduring that emotional upheaval on the big rappel had taken its toll. I'd accomplished what I needed to. I'd pushed past my fear, proved to myself that I could physically do this crazy thing, and finally seen slot canyons up close and personal. My body ached, my hand felt like it was broken, and I was done.

I resolved to meet my cohorts in the morning and tell them I was going no farther. After my ridiculous behavior in the latter part of the day, I figured they'd probably cheer as soon as they were out of earshot. As I drifted off to sleep, that was my game plan for the next day.

It really was.

A NIGHTMARE WOKE ME AT 4 A.M., and finding sleep again was impossible. In the dark, I sat on the corner of the bed for a while, waiting for the light of day and remembering the conclusion I'd come to last night.

Then I sighed and packed my gear bag. Quit? What was I thinking?

When Payne and I met in the parking lot, he told me he hadn't slept well either, that he'd had dreams of precipices all night. It was barely light out and very cold, and we were all uncharacteristically quiet as we drove toward our final destination: Battle Creek. Jonathan told us we'd do at least five rappels today, all of them through waterfalls. And yesterday, he'd told us to pack the rappelling gear at the top of our backpacks. I figured it was because we'd been taking too long to get to our gear.

Payne and Red piled into the truck, while I told Jonathan I needed to run to the restroom. On my return, I caught him rifling through my pack. He said he was just "making adjustments."

The access to Battle Creek by vehicle was rough, steep, and bumpy. There were a number of cattle gates to open and close. Since I was in the front passenger seat, that became *my* job.

One gate was rusty and stuck, and as I heaved on it with both hands, I felt something bite into my thumb and bright red blood spurted into the air. A Chinese ribbon flew out of my mouth when I looked at my hand. The slice in my thumb was deep, and there was an alarming amount of blood. The cut was exactly where my thumb would have to lock down on the rope.

Dammit! I opened the gate, then closed it after the truck passed through, swearing the whole time. My two steps forward on the road to redemption were about to be erased.

"Jonathan," I said when I climbed back into the truck, "Do you have a Band-Aid?" I showed him my thumb. Blood had already started coagulating on the back of my hand and inside my palm. It looked really bad. "Figures," I heard Red mutter. Payne leaned forward and inspected the wound.

"When was your last tetanus shot?" he asked.

"July 1996," I answered, instantly recalling my terrible horseback riding accident and the resulting hospital trauma.

"You should be OK," he said and sat back. I liked Payne. No nonsense. No drama. Reliable. If he were a horse, I would have bought him.

This was day three. Jonathan's earlier words echoed in my head: "On day three I will be a liability," he'd said. I couldn't imagine the travails we were in for today.

"Our hike to the canyon," he explained, "is not difficult, just picky. Janice, you lead. Follow the creek to the end."

The creek was a shallow, narrow little rivulet, pleasant enough except that it required crisscrossing icy waters, stepping over debris, scrambling over rocks. The hike was a good hour at least, and tiring. And at the end was a waterfall. How that little creek could generate such a volume of water was a mystery to me, but there it was—our first rappel.

"Get your dry suits on," said Jonathan. "I'm going to leave you now. When I come back, I want you all at the bottom of the first rappel." Jonathan gave us some quick tips about getting the dry suit gaskets over our heads. The suits, he explained, were worth more than $2,000 apiece, so would we please be careful with them? I looked at mine—a yellow, blue, and red patchwork rubber extravaganza that looked like a panel from the Partridge Family bus. Red quickly zipped into his wet suit top, while Payne and I groaned and pulled and eventually had to help each other get the damned things on.

Red waited for us, but his impatience overcame his team spirit. He set the ropes, pulled them through his Pirana, and disappeared. With my thumb bleeding and useless, it took me a little while longer to get ready. Payne stood by patiently. *Where's Jonathan?* I kept thinking. *If he went off for a pee, he should be back by now.*

Digging around inside my backpack with a bleeding thumb wasn't resulting in anything except a bloodstained interior. I didn't like this one bit. We were about to descend through waterfalls into deep water and Jonathan was nowhere to be seen. But then came the real pièce de résistance: Jonathan had gone into our packs and *removed* equipment. In my case he had taken my Pirana, my safety tether, and my ascenders. All I had left were my harness, one carabiner, and an autoblock. Payne's Pirana was gone too, although he had a few more things to work with than I did. Big Red's gear was pretty much intact.

When Jonathan returned, I confronted him. He smiled. "What is your alternative to the rappelling device?" he asked me. I knew the answer but didn't want to admit it.

"The Munter hitch," I said sheepishly. Yes, I had practiced it all night, but it is the simplest twist of a rope you have ever seen. This was supposed to support all my weight? Jonathan got on rope and, just like that, disappeared from sight.

"Off rope!" I heard him call.

I tied and retied that hitch. "Payne, is this right?" Payne just shrugged. "Janice," he said, "I'm not entirely sure." Eventually, Jonathan called up to ask what was taking so long. I looked at Payne and shook my head.

Payne called down, "We're dealing with some indecision at the moment."

Jonathan did not observe me as I tied the final Munter hitch, or at least I didn't see him. I asked Payne what he thought. "Janice," he said, "I can't tell you one way or another."

So when I laid my weight on that rope, on the knot I had tied to preserve my own life, I had no idea whether it would hold or not. It was, in retrospect, the biggest leap of faith I have ever taken.

Crashing water and my ragged, raspy breathing—that's what I heard when I stepped off the edge, not fully trusting that the simple hitch would hold. When it did, a surge of adrenaline made my smile so big I thought it would crack my face in half.

Down I went, along a narrow chute filled with flowing water and bright green algae. The rock face suddenly changed angles, and I shouted down to Jonathan.

"What should I do?"

"I could tell you," he answered, "but that would rob you of the learning experience." I shook my head and chuckled. This was *such* a Jonathan answer.

Meanwhile, I was busy feeling that now familiar moment when one wrong step would send me flying into the rock face. I looked around, changed the position of my feet, didn't fight gravity, and allowed myself to be taken where the rope dictated. It was controlled, quiet, and just fine. I laughed. I was having the time of my life! Everything was working and this canyon was exquisite. For the last two days, I'd listened to my heartbeat thudding in my ears. Now, the sound of the water was everywhere. Spray off the rocks rained on my face. I stopped for a moment to feel this: I'd suddenly shifted to somewhere new.

When I landed in the pool below, the waterfall pummeled my head and I had to work to get free of its force. If the water flow were higher and stronger, a person trapped there could die. I felt enormous awe and respect for the forces of nature I was navigating.

Jonathan said only four things to me after that. The first one was: "That was your homework assignment, Janice. You were supposed to know the Munter in your sleep."

We rappelled through some more waterfalls in the canyon and everything was perfect. Just perfect. The canyon narrowed and

the waterfalls became fiercer. I could barely see the blue sky overhead, and the sun—even though I could tell it was shining—wasn't
warming the canyon. The water was *so* cold. Even through the dry
suit I could feel it. I wasn't worried about hypothermia, though.
As cold as I was, I was bone dry inside that $2,000 rubber-and-
latex fashion statement. Red's wetsuit top should have been keeping him comfortable, but he started showing signs of distress early.
Jonathan was concerned. Red confessed that he'd left his cotton
T-shirt on underneath. *Now who's the asshole,* I thought.

Payne looked at Red's hands and asked him a few questions.
Red shivered uncontrollably and kept looking down-canyon as
if he were getting ready to jump. "We need to get him out of here
and into the sunlight," Payne said. I knew we had two or three
rappels to go and one was just below us. There was no need to
down-climb or rope our way, there was a natural waterslide carved
into the rock. Down we went on our butts—*whoosh!* I felt a little bad that I was having such a wonderful time while Red was
suffering, but it felt *so good* finally to be free of the fear that had
been nipping at my heels since the beginning of this adventure.

At the next rappel, it appeared that we could do it in two stages
or in one, so Payne and I began to discuss. Red groaned. "Let's
go!" he shouted.

"Just wait a minute," I snapped. "You want this done fast, or
you want it done right?"

"I'm going," he pronounced, and prepared to jump into a deep
pool below. He was literally about to take a dive when I grabbed
his backpack and pulled him off balance.

"If you want to kill yourself, go ahead," I said, "but you've got
all the extra gear, so hand them over before you jump."

"Fuck you," he said but complied. I took an extra rope, too, just in case, and Red leaped. I saw what he saw—daylight on the canyon floor, just one more rappel away.

"How are you going to get out of that pool, Red?" I called down. "Now you're going to get even colder, bobbing around in that water."

Payne and I were looking desperately for something we could use to anchor the rope. Whatever bolts had once been there were gone, and there were no viable trees. The only thing that looked even remotely possible was a chockstone the size of a large exercise ball. I pushed on it and pulled and looked at the amount of debris around it. "I don't know, Payne," I said, "it could give way."

"Come onnnnnnn!" I heard Red wailing below. Over the last two days, Payne and I had demonstrated our ultraconservative approach to setting the ropes, whereas Red preferred to make quick decisions and get on with things. You need both approaches in canyoneering, but knowing that we needed to hurry up was pushing me outside of my comfort zone. I tied an "eight on a bight," and the second thing Jonathan said to me was, "That is an unacceptable knot." I silently blamed my swollen hand and my cold fingers, but I tied it again and received no admonition. Everything seemed to be taking forever.

Suddenly, Red shouted from below, *"Bolts!"*

We turned to see him bobbing next to a ledge, and sure enough, there were two bolts about five feet above his head. We abandoned the chockstone and threw him a rope. He managed to get himself on the ledge—a completely precarious position, considering the water was spilling over it with impressive force— and set a double rope. He quickly rappelled down into the third pool, the last pool of the day. I watched as he thrashed his way out of the water and the narrow canyon and into a wide bright spot and the blessed sun.

Payne and I jumped into the second pool and paddled our way over to the rope. This was going to be my last rappel, so I decided to go as slowly as I could. Red was safely out of the water and warming himself in the sun, so I was free to indulge. Payne set the ropes and the third thing Jonathan said to me was, "Please reach up and lock that carabiner before you trust your life to it."

"Payne!" I chided. Throughout our adventure he'd consistently forgotten to lock the carabiners and was being fined by Jonathan in the process. Payne shook his head. "Jeez," he said, "It's up to 50 bucks!"

A few twists of the lock and the carabiner was safe. Soon I would be back on solid ground, but for now, I made my way down the rope as slowly as I could, listening to the roar of the water, smelling the bright, clean air, feeling the needles of water sting my face, the pain of the rope as it pressed against the cut on my thumb. I hung on as the water pushed and slapped against me. I breathed in and out, in and out. Over and over again. I looked up-canyon one last time. Everything was exquisite and real and pure. I felt tears coming, and this time I let them.

This is what I came for, what I'd waited my whole life to see.

On the little sandy piece of sunlight, after lunch and sufficient warming, we began our hike through the wash, back to civilization.

The fourth and final thing Jonathan said to me was, "Keep an eye out for the red rope!" I groaned. I guess I really *had* laid down the gauntlet the other day. We were going to have to *ascend* out of the canyon.

The hike wasn't bad—only a few steep spots—and Red found the infamous rope in short order. I'm going to say it was a 100-foot rock face and stick to that story. It looked a lot higher. Red went first, with the only set of ascenders left to us by the marauding Jonathan. Red got up there pretty quickly and then lowered the ascenders. I was next.

I decided I would try to be gracious and not make up any new words this time. That didn't last long. I could not even stand up in the makeshift stirrup. Absolutely nothing was happening with my legs. I thought that sheer stubbornness would get me out of there, but my legs were unimpressed. They went on strike.

Jonathan told Payne to remove my pack, and with that 35-pound albatross off my back I began to ascend, and wasn't doing a bad job of it either. Three-quarters of the way up I stopped to rest, and a hummingbird came to visit. It hovered in front of my face and made eye contact, looking and wondering what I was and what on earth I was doing there. It was a reminder to slow down and appreciate every moment of what I was doing. So I did.

The last part of the ascent was the hardest, over a crag and a bush to a tiny ledge only big enough for a curled-up body. Above that, another small ascension. Big Red was already gone, having found the "hidden" ascenders in his pack. I sent my ascenders down to Payne and settled in for a long wait.

I sat on that wet, narrow, sandy ledge in a fetal position and looked all around the canyon, occasional butterflies swarming in my stomach if my eyes happened to fall on the precipice near my feet. I was grateful for the time alone to absorb all that had happened to me in the last three days. With my cheek against the cold stone of the canyon, I realized that one of the things Jonathan had told us on day one was true. In almost all cases, it's important to tie a small knot at the end of the rope before you throw it. This is so you don't accidentally rappel off the rope into space, especially if you've guessed at the distance and are wrong. Having a knot at the end of your rope keeps you from danger, from making a tragic mistake. I thought about my emotional rope and how on day one my personal knot was so close to my hand. After three days, how far down the rope had it moved, I wondered? How far was I willing to stray from knowing with certainty that I was safe?

By navigating the canyons on a rope, I had connected to Zion in a new way and had been privileged to see a few of its secret places. And I discovered a few hidden places of my own.

Before this trip, I hadn't known how hard it would be to summon courage or sustain it. It would take me a long time to figure out what happened that day on the big drop, to understand exactly what I lost and what I gained in those terrifying moments. Who I was then was not the person I would become when I walked out of this canyon.

But for now it was enough to sit curled up on that ledge. And wait.

We can never be certain of our courage till we have faced danger. —François, duc de La Rochefoucauld

SO MY FASCINATION WITH FEAR—or, more appropriately, how to take action in spite of it—came as a result of that dramatic moment on the edge of the big cliff deep inside the slot canyons of Utah. Why, if I had all the skills needed to navigate that particular drop, did I suddenly and inexplicably freeze? What was that fierce and terrifying sense of internal disintegration, as if I were a ball of yarn unraveling at a hundred miles an hour? As the days, weeks, and months passed, I became quietly obsessed with wanting to know what happened in that moment when fear had rendered me as immovable as the stone I stood upon, yet I was somehow able to move anyway. Was that what it meant to be brave?

It turns out that courage is an elusive concept even for much greater minds than mine. In 1918, American philosopher William Ernest Hocking (1873–1966) wrote a classic piece on soldiering and the difficulties new soldiers face when learning how to be brave. Many of them suffer, Hocking said, from a "fear of fear." These soldiers, Hocking wrote, hope that they will be able to rise to the occasion when it presents itself, but secretly they are not sure they will. Hocking goes on to say something that should make us all feel better, whether our fear is of public speaking or getting our hearts broken: "The fact is, no one knows in advance how he is going to behave in an emergency. But one thing can be said with entire confidence—and this should be of some service to those who fancy that their being afraid will mark them out from their comrades—*everybody fears.*"

Everybody fears. Faced with a threat, soldiers respond with the same trembling, heavy breathing, and narrowed vision as most of us would when on a high-ropes team-building exercise or standing our ground against a ferocious dog or speaking in front of a throng of people. The difference is that soldiers experience it every day, either in combat or in military training. They have no choice *but* to exercise and strengthen their capacity for courage. Hocking asserts that the physical manifestations of fear can "be brought under control, but as in most other matters, *after having been experienced,* and by the aid of experience—not before."

Practice, then, helps *everyone* become stronger, and braver, and more competent. Perhaps the most comforting thing Hocking shares, especially to those of us who secretly believe we're cowards, is this: "Familiarity with the same dangers eventually leaves the human animal unmoved. One's nerves no longer quiver; the conscious and constant effort to keep control over one's self is successful in the end. Therein lies the secret of all . . . courage. Men are not born brave; they become brave."

Why does this even matter? Very few of us lie awake at night wondering if we're courageous. We're more likely to be asking ourselves if we're competent, good parents, attractive, too big, too small, smart enough, rich enough. Bravery isn't typically a topic that springs to mind when we review our list of attributes and deficits. Yet everyone would like to think of him- or herself as brave, as a person capable of doing the hard and fearsome thing when it becomes necessary to do so.

But fear—real fear—is a formidable enemy. When I experienced it on the big rappel in Utah, it was excruciating. And yet I keep chasing after that feeling, testing myself, trying new things. For the record, I'm not a thrill seeker. I don't even like cold water when I'm brushing my teeth. I've been perfectly content to eat a pizza, take a bike ride with the kids, then go to bed at nine. So what is it, then, this obsession with pushing myself to the edge?

I think I have finally learned that without jamming that personal envelope to the fringes, I will become complacent. If I retreat from challenges, time's lumbering shadow will eventually overtake me and I'll suddenly find myself unable even to climb a ladder to clean the gutters. The context of the challenge is immaterial. Afraid of conflict? Afraid of commitment? Afraid of rain? *Your* challenge is the one you need to address. What matters is that you face it with conviction, and you face it before fear darkens too many windows inside your heart.

Facing physical fears is in many ways easier than facing psychological ones. Physical fear is tangible: *If I step off this cliff without tying my knot correctly I will die.* There's no predictable consequence for laying your heart out on the table, even though underneath it might be a chasm full of fear. In front of a 200-foot sheer cliff, it makes sense to be afraid. Who wouldn't be? There, you have a really concrete, obvious monster to overcome. But when you have to psych yourself up to do something in daily life, and that something makes you sick to your stomach or sets your knees to knocking, it's hard to know *exactly* where the fear originates. It becomes easier to avoid it altogether, because, frankly, there's no one on the outside observing what's happening on the inside. You can fail, and fail, and fail, and who will be the wiser? How many people do you know who have never asked for a raise, even though they deserved one, simply because they were afraid of hearing "no"? How can one word carry so much power and invoke so much fear? How can we so easily talk ourselves out of doing the things we know we must do?

Opportunities to be courageous abound in daily life, but most of us become pretty good at avoiding them as deliberately as we would a hornet's nest. Perhaps for me the worst home-based fear of all was riding Brazen again after the 1996 accident, which was so bad the doctors told me I'd walk like a penguin for the rest of my life. Getting "back on the horse" was literal but also metaphorical: having to stand up, dust myself off, and put myself at risk again wasn't a situation confined just to a four-legged beast and a saddle. In the middle of trying to overcome the trauma of that riding accident, I realized it was just a more dramatic version of all the other difficult things I had to deal with in my life. It's *hard* to put your heart out there after it's been broken, to trust after you've been deceived, to believe in yourself after you've failed. Slithering down into a narrow slot canyon was in many ways preferable to standing up to my awful board chair "Dee," but with each challenge I become a little more adept. Still, I've never quite overcome the knots in my stomach or the shaking hands or the sinking feeling right before taking the leap—whatever that leap is. Will I ever?

I don't know, but I do know that courage—real courage, where there is fear and danger and risk involved—isn't easily plucked from amid a riot of emotions or pulled out of some fleeting or extended desperation to understand what to do at the critical moment. Courageous action happens *in spite* of doubts and insecurities and bewilderment. It happens like the fast-forward blossoming of a flower—breathtaking and unstoppable. But how do we become courageous? Can we practice to be brave?

I think we can. Courage is like a muscle. And like any other muscle, it must be exercised before it will be strong and poised to do the heavy lifting when fear attempts to weigh us down. It's foolish to think that without some prior preparation, courage will simply find us, unbidden, when we're in a clinch and need it to power us through. That's like spending your whole life sitting on the couch watching TV and then expecting to spring up suddenly one day and run a marathon.

Some philosophers say courage is won only in the face of real peril, when what you're about to do will most likely cost you your life, or at least result in the kind of pain and suffering best left to martyrs. Other writers think that sticking to a diet or overcoming a dislike for brussels sprouts is courageous. There's a wide road connecting these two extremes and somewhere in the middle is where average people like you and me can create opportunities to discover what we're made of, to find out if we are indeed brave when it counts.

Navigating through difficult work obstacles that *must* end in success can be as nerve-racking as paddling through rapids. Facing up to a demanding boss or dealing with bad personal relationships, even disciplining a beloved child, can be harder than stepping off a cliff, but every time we push ourselves through those trials we find it easier to deal with and get through the next.

A Gallup poll conducted in 2001 found that among a sample of 1,000 American adults, the top 13 fears were these: snakes (51 percent); public speaking (40 percent); heights (36 percent); being closed in a small space (34 percent); spiders and insects (27 percent); needles and getting shots (21 percent); mice (20 percent); flying on an airplane (18 percent); dogs (11 percent); thunder and lightning (11 percent); crowds (11 percent); going to the doctor (9 percent); the dark (5 percent). With the exception of going to the doctor, women overwhelmingly expressed a higher level of fear in all categories than men did. Look carefully at the list: five are part and parcel of the natural world; three are potentially part of everyone's work environment; and two are rather mundane things that aren't life-threatening in any way (going to the doctor, getting shots). Note that none of these fears is a significant threat to life and limb (unless you happen to get on the wrong plane, kiss a poisonous snake, or pet the wrong dog). Having a fear of cancer makes more sense than a fear of going to the doctor. If you share any of the "Top 13" fears, this is a great place to start figuring out how to overcome them. Three of these common fears are mine as well—stinging insects, heights, and getting shots. For me, attacking the fear of heights helped lessen my fear of the other two. The canyons put them in their place.

Mainstream North American culture seems to take every detour it can around discomfort and fear, but in many cultures, one's transition from child to adult requires a test to display evidence of bravery, of self-determination, of the ability to endure suffering. Among the Maasai of East Africa, the rite of passage to adulthood for adolescent boys used to involve roaming the African plains alone, armed only with a spear, searching for a lion to kill. Confronting a lion with nothing but a spear and a sackful of conviction has to be petrifying, but that was the only acceptable way boys could "prove" they were worthy of being called men. Due to declining lion populations, this ritual is now discouraged, but the Maasai have replaced it with other tests of skill, recognizing the value of the ritualized trial.

For Luiseño Indian boys in southern California, the rite of passage involved lying on red ant mounds for long periods of time. They proved they were fit for grown-up status by not crying out in pain as they were tormented by insect bites. Perhaps this was more a test of endurance than bravery, but it still required inner resolve, fortitude, and tenacity in order to succeed at the task and move from one rank to the next.

And on Pentecost Island in the South Pacific, the indigenous people still practice a ritual rite of passage (and an offering of gratitude for a good harvest) called land diving (the inspiration for modern bungee jumping). Adolescent boys and young men prove their manhood by climbing rickety 60- to 100-foot towers made of tree branches, then tying vines around both ankles, attaching the vines to the tower, and diving straight toward the ground. This makes my whole Munter hitch meltdown pale by comparison. Ideally, the vines should deposit the jumper just inches above the ground, but sometimes the vines are too long and the diver makes contact with the land. Sometimes the vines are too short and the diver doesn't pass the test. And sometimes, the vines break. It is a truly terrifying and genuinely dangerous rite of passage, but like all the others, it's symbolic of the need we all feel to have the inner resources to be brave when it counts.

Anthills and vines and spears are a bit extreme, but there's an important lesson embedded within every one of these intense rites of passage. Life—these rituals seem to imply—is full of pain and suffering, so you better show us you can handle them both before we pronounce you ready for the responsibilities of adulthood.

Except for military training, many cultures now seem to have abandoned ritualized opportunities for helping their members develop bravery or learn to accept that suffering and fear, no matter how much we try to avoid them, are a part of life. Rituals and practice help us learn to navigate gracefully the territory of fear—important, because at some point or another, we will all be dwelling there.

Here's what Lewis Glenn, former vice president for safety at Outward Bound USA, says about courage: "Two things come to mind: presence and focus in the moment. Having to overcome a fearful obstacle allows us and compels us to be present in the moment in a way we usually can't or won't be. . . . It's a matter of commitment also: 'I'm going to do this.' Two things that define the experience: visceral commitment, and the realization that one is existentially alone."

Existentially alone. Thinking back on my travels, I know that he's right. Yet far from being a depressing or hopeless idea, understanding that we are existentially alone is actually an invitation to understand ourselves better—what we can and cannot do, what we're capable of in our core. It's a challenge to all of us to get off the riding lawn mower and into the woods. A reminder to drop the Wii and get into the boxing ring for real. To go beyond walking the dog at a leisurely pace and drive a team of dogs across the Yukon instead.

The key is to resist being discouraged by the initial discomfort and to keep pushing through to the ultimate goal—freedom from the fear that is holding you back, whether that fear is of ending a bad relationship or of skydiving. It's not that you will banish all traces of fear—you won't—but you'll get to the point where fear can't stop you the way it wants to. The first step can take a really long time. Look at me—13 visits to southern Utah before I finally summoned the nerve to get on a rope. But here's something important to think about. Rappelling into slot canyons wasn't a random choice. I didn't seek that danger for thrills. For more than 20 years I'd wanted to experience a slot canyon from the inside. In order to do that, I had to go eyeball to eyeball with the fear of heights that was firmly rooted between my dream and me. Those canyons sometimes tore my emotional fabric apart, and what got stitched back together was different, my seams no longer likely to split apart at the slightest tension. Heights *still* make me quiver, but no longer will fear or discomfort unravel the threads of my resolve to do the thing I'm setting out to do.

Winston Churchill and Aristotle both believed that of all human virtues, courage is the enforcing one, the one that guarantees the others, and therefore the one most critical to develop. Lest you think Churchill was predisposed to be brave, know that as a boy he was unhealthy, utterly unremarkable in academic accomplishments, and suffered from a speech impediment. Churchill understood the necessity of testing himself, and when the time came for him to rescue his country from war, his self-imposed and harsh lessons had readied him for victory.

Churchill believed that it should be an ongoing principle of one's life to be curious and daring and to seek opportunities in normal life to be courageous. Long before he became prime minister of England, Churchill had prepared himself for the unexpected and the unknown by reading everything he could get his hands on and by experiencing almost every visceral challenge available to a man at that time. He was a combat soldier in the far reaches of the British Empire, a war correspondent, a prisoner of war (and successful escapee) while a journalist in the Boer War, member of Parliament, first lord of the Admiralty, minister of munitions, secretary of state for war, secretary of state for air, colonial secretary, chancellor of the exchequer, prime minister, and a Nobel Prize winner in literature. Not bad for a puny, sickly boy who suffered the regular attention of bullies. Churchill didn't just jump up one day from behind his desk and become a great leader and courageous man. He did what Hocking described—he *learned* how to become brave.

Churchill is such a compelling example of courage that most of us would never aspire to his inestimable accomplishments. Yet all of us have the opportunity, somewhere in our lives, to make courageous decisions that might change things forever. Take Juliette

Gordon Low, who was born in 1860 to an influential family in provincial Savannah, Georgia. Juliette showed exceptional talent as an artist and thinker, but her formal education did little to encourage these gifts. She was a girl, after all, and in that era, her education was considered far less important than her brother's. Plagued by ear infections, Juliette was mostly deaf in one ear when, at 26, she married a man who would take her to England. The marriage would ultimately fail, and perhaps as a portent to this unhappy ending, a grain of "good luck" rice thrown at the wedding became lodged in Juliette's one working ear. The doctor who tried to remove it punctured her eardrum and for the rest of her life, Juliette was almost completely deaf.

Her marriage ended in 1905, and in 1912, at the age of 52, Juliette met Lord and Lady Baden Powell, founders of the scouting movement in England. They introduced her to the idea of a program that could have a positive impact on the integrity, ability, and capability of youth. Juliette suddenly knew what she would do with the rest of her life.

After an ocean crossing back to the United States, she announced, "I've got something for the girls of Savannah, and all of America and all the world, and we start it tonight." That "something" would ultimately become the Girl Scouts of the United States of America, an organization devoted to helping girls from every faction of life to grow strong and self-reliant through a progressive program of skill building, risk taking, and community service.

One might question why this is considered brave, but remember that in 1912, in the early 20th-century American South, women were expected to "know their place." They were expected to be demure and deferential. Imagine the raised eyebrows when

Juliette announced she was taking her girls into the woods for a few days so they could learn survival skills. Girls could also earn Girl Scout badges in the male-dominated realms of automotive repair and airplane navigation, earning scorn from some and bemused looks from others. Juliette encouraged girls to be physically active, despite the restrictions in place at the time. In fact, Girl Scouts could play basketball outdoors only if there were curtains around the court to shield viewers from the sight of females playing in their bloomers. Scandalous!

Aside from the badges, the cookouts, the camping trips, the good deeds done in the community, girls came away with something few of them would have had otherwise: self-determination and the conviction that they could shape their own destiny.

Juliette died of breast cancer at the age of 67, having kept the disease a secret so as not to divert attention from the Girl Scout movement. Throughout her life, she never succumbed to criticism or apathy. She used her deafness to her advantage, refusing to hear or acknowledge the word "no," especially when it came to raising money or recruiting volunteers. Think about it: Juliette was a divorcee, "older," handicapped, and had breast cancer, yet she changed the landscape of the future for girls and women in the United States forever. She embodied the motto she taught her girls: "Every time you show your courage, it grows."

Our greatest teachers are the terrible moments when we think we can't do the thing we need to do, when pain and fear and doubt join hands to choke the spirit out of us. But those are our finest moments, when we're called upon to summon courage. They give us the confidence to face daily life and losses with a kind of steadiness we hadn't had before.

Every day at work I think about how my canyoneering instructor, Jonathan, patiently and from a distance, guided me through a minefield of fear, preparing me for the last critical step I had to take alone. When I become frustrated by employees who won't take risks, I put them in the context of the canyon, remember how afraid I'd been, and offer them what Jonathan had offered me—a hand to hold at the beginning, a way to practice new skills, then a push forward at the decisive moment.

A few years after my canyoneering adventure, I went to Ireland to gallop horses at breakneck speed across the countryside—and not because I thought it would be fun. Ever since my riding accident on Brazen, fear had taken a permanent seat in my saddle, riding double with me wherever I went, making sure all my equine outings were fraught with worry. In Ireland, jumping over ditches, up and down banks, into and out of streams, and over fences bigger than anything I'd ever faced was meant to unseat that fear, to throw it to the ground and trample it, to leave it behind in the dust of pounding hooves. If I could succeed at that, I knew my regular rides at home would be what they used to be before the accident—a deeply satisfying connection with the natural world.

Learning to deal with fear also brought an unanticipated reward—comfort with ambiguity. Very few things in life go according to plan; there are always surprises along the way. The year I turned 50 I lost my job after a successful 20-year career as a CEO. It was the kind of derailment that could have flooded me with fear and panic and rendered me incapable of rational thought. But when I learned of this impending job loss, instincts took over—instincts that had been honed and hardened by nine trips into the canyons—allowing me to remain calm and really *think* about what to do next. All of my solo travels, the time I had alone to really think about things and push myself out of my comfort zone, opened a door to the path beyond fear. Freedom like that comes only from being able to be relaxed with uncertainty, to let go of expectations and accept what is happening *now* for what it *is*, not what you think it should be or is supposed to be. Wrestling with fear over and over again built the muscle I needed to handle a harsh reality not with dread but with excitement for all that a new future might bring.

We may not ever conquer a fear, but we can learn to negotiate with it. To live a life full of possibility instead of regret, we need to be vigilant every day, to remember to say yes instead of no. It's the only way to nurture the seed of our individual potential. We must remember that it is not enough to be brave just once—or just in the big, dramatic moments where anyone in their right mind would be scared out of their wits—but to be brave on a small scale as well. If you commit to being courageous, you'll begin to appreciate the quiet blessings that come to you every day. You'll make better decisions and inspire others. You'll leave a legacy. When you become better, stronger, and braver, everyone wins.

If life's full experience is the wild and unstoppable arc of a pendulum, who wants to live in the middle? Pushing ourselves to the point of feeling fear, shaking off discomfort and summoning courage, challenging ourselves in a way that makes us feel we might die—*that* is what it means to live. And make no mistake, it changes us forever.

At the end of our days, when we look back on our lives, what do we want to remember? A comfortable life lived in the middle?

Theodore Roosevelt had a thought about people who live that way. "Poor spirits," he called them, "who neither enjoy nor suffer much because they live in that gray twilight that knows neither victory nor defeat." A later Roosevelt, First Lady Eleanor, advised, "Do one thing every day that scares you." Facing fear, negotiating with it, winning now and then, means we live as we are meant to, with gusto and uncertainty and the occasional wild and breathless ride. But to be brave like this will take a lifetime of practice. It will take a promise, a pledge, a *commitment,* to never, *ever* let fear win.

EXERCISES

WHY COURAGE?

Moving out of the reality we're in and into the reality we want will take courage. If it didn't, we'd have the life we want already. Courage isn't easily summoned or easily sustained, yet there's one thing that's certain: we'll all need at one time or another to be brave when it counts.

Through introspection (see chapter 4), you may have discovered one or two obstacles you wish to overcome, and in doing so, you'll have to take risks and be brave, even when it's scary.

EXERCISES IN COURAGE

Identify a Goal

What have you always wanted to do but keep making excuses for not doing? There are probably a number of things, but pick the one that has real meaning to you. For me, it was going into slot canyons. It will be something different for you. Identify at least one big thing you'd like to overcome.

Take Baby Steps

I don't recommend trying to tackle your biggest fear on your first foray. It's like weight lifting. In order to be able to lift 100 pounds, you first have to be able to lift 5, then 10, then 20, and so on. It's the same with courage. If courage is a muscle, you don't want to sprain it too soon.

One Thing Leads to Another

Stress Exposure Training (SET) is used a lot in military and par-amilitary training. SET takes the big, scary thing and breaks it down into manageable pieces. If the big, scary thing is jumping out of an airplane, first acclimate yourself to heights by standing on a small ladder, then tackle a climbing wall, then try a zip line. These things might be really frightening or they might just be uncomfortable, but what you're doing is exercising your capacity to take action even when you're scared. By the time you're ready to jump out of a plane, you'll be able to take the leap despite feeling frightened.

Be Supportive of Yourself

You can't really rush this process, and you shouldn't be discouraged if you're not successful right away. It's the *trying* that counts. In the short term, it really doesn't matter if you succeed or fail. Every time you go back to give it another go, you're building your courage muscle.

Practice on a Small Stage

Emotional courage is harder to talk about because it's not tangible. Sometimes it will require you to be quiet, and sometimes it will require that you speak out. Don't wait until the moment of truth arrives, when everything rides on your decision to speak or be silent. Begin practicing in situations where there's not so much on the line. Do this in staff meetings, in family discussions, or conversations with friends. Practice being quiet and practice speaking up. Use what you will learn in the solitude exercises (chapter 3) to notice how you feel when you either lean against or flow with your instincts. Push yourself a little bit into that place you avoid going. If friends are talking about other friends in a way you don't like, say that you'd prefer they not do that. Speak respectfully and assuredly, knowing that you are doing the right thing, even though your heart may be pounding and everyone may be uncomfortable for a little while. Don't be discouraged: no transformation comes from a place of comfort.

EXERCISES TOWARD COURAGE

Flexing your courage muscle is as important as regular exercise if you want to live the fuller, more rewarding life you seek. Staying committed to your goals and then taking action to reach them are essential for a well-lived, satisfying life.

Let It Be Known

Whatever you decide to do, broadcast your intention to do it: "By the end of this year, I will jump out of a plane." Tell everyone and anyone who will listen. Repeat to them why it's important to you to do this thing. Stating it aloud reinforces it for you and lays down a kind of gauntlet. It's not so easy to back out once you've told half your hometown that you'll be dangling from a parachute by the time Christmas rolls around.

Grab a Buddy

Unlike solitude (chapter 3) and introspection (chapter 4), courage can be practiced with other people. Sometimes it's easier to fight back fear when you're buoyed by camaraderie and support. It's also more likely you'll go through with it: once you've made a commitment to and with someone else, it's harder to back out.

Deconstruct

After your big moment is over, spend some time alone for thoughtful pause: How did you feel in the worst of it? What made you almost give up? What made you go forward? What were you thinking in the moments before and after you stepped over the fear? This introspection is a critical piece of understanding where your courage comes from and how it can be built going forward. Your exercises in solitude (chapter 3) and introspection (chapter 4) have prepared you for this by teaching you how to *notice*.

Make a Map

At least once a year, survey your life and identify any scary obstacles forming roadblocks to your intended destination. Resolve to overcome them before the year is out. And even if you have found the secret to happiness and are perfectly content, commit to doing something scary once a year, just to make sure the courage inside you hasn't withered up and blown away like dandelion fluff on the breeze.

CHAPTER THREE

SOLITUDE

Solitude had delivered to me a moment of grace, a secret glimpse into what it means and how it feels to be completely connected to life and everything in it.

I'D ORDERED A BIGGER RENTAL CAR, but that was now beside the point. How in the world was I going to get three suitcases into this tiny blue convertible? Even the smallest of my bags—perfectly sized for an airplane overhead bin—wouldn't fit in the trunk. And my biggest bag—a yellow hard-sider the color and size of a life raft—wouldn't fit anywhere. The prospect of schlepping everything *back* from the parking lot to the rental desk at San Francisco airport filled me with dread; the line there had already cost me two hours, and if I had to drag these bags *one more minute* I was going to start saying things unfit for civilized people to hear.

"Dammit!" I shouted. Even with the front seats pulled all the way to the dashboard, I could barely pass a leg into the backseat, let alone fit luggage in there. On the plus side, the big yellow suitcase made an excellent emergency settee, and I sat there think-ing, tapping one foot on the oil-stained black pavement.

Like the proverbial lightbulb, a solution suddenly flashed in my head. Packed inside one of the suitcases were some bungee cords (in case an overpacked bag exploded) and—*eureka!*—the answer. First, though, the convertible top needed to come down. That way I could throw the big suitcase in the back, and the sec-ond largest in the passenger seat. The smallest suitcase I'd shove in the trunk, securing it there with bungee cords and incantations.

This luggage trifecta was getting ridiculous. Hauling all this crap around was hurting my shoulders and aggravating the bone spurs in my neck. Plus, it was difficult and awkward. What the hell did I bring anyway? Jimmy Hoffa's body? All the "just in case" items—some dress-up outfits, high heels, bathing suits in three different styles, face cloths, jewelry, five paperback books, magazines I hadn't gotten around to reading—would be jettisoned for future trips. What did I think I was going to need those black high heels for? And hiking doesn't require the ornamentation of earrings, bracelets, and necklaces. Next time, I promised myself, I was going to pack only what I could carry easily. That would be all well and good for the future, but for this trip I was stuck with the consequences of my inefficient packing. What a relief it would be, finally, just to grab a bag and go.

Point Reyes National Seashore was my destination, but San Francisco traffic conspired to keep me from arriving there on time. With all the stopping and starting and occasional gridlock I could gaze around, slowly opening locked-away memories. I hadn't been in San Francisco for a very long time. There was Golden Gate Park. The Presidio. The bay. And there, ahead of me, on an unusually vivid day, was the Golden Gate Bridge. Off to the right was Alcatraz. I smiled at them the way you'd smile at an old book you knew from childhood, and as with that warm memory, there was a melancholy too, a strange sort of sadness. All of my San Francisco recollections were attached in some way and at different times to significant people who were no longer in my life. And suddenly I wished—for the first time in a long time—that I wasn't taking this trip alone.

Highway 101 along the coast is a narrow gantlet of relentless twists and turns, requiring a two-handed grip on the wheel at all times. Only occasionally on the rare, straight pieces of road was I able to steal glances at the Pacific Ocean sprawled out under the cloud-streaked blue sky. At a beach access I parked the car and walked to the water. Even the pounding of the waves and the smell of the ocean didn't dissipate that lingering sadness. *Go away! I want to think about the water and the sand and the sun, not be stuck in some memory that no longer matters.*

The smell of the Pacific Ocean is so different from other oceans, in a way I can never explain. It was part of my childhood on the West Coast, just outside Vancouver, British Columbia. Sans shoes, I walked in the deep, rough sand until the water's edge made it hard and ready for the tide. The water was so cold. Fragments of kelp, seaweed, and grass rushed past my ankles in the waves swirling around my feet. As a little girl, I was afraid of kelp, afraid when I looked over the side of my dad's rowboat and saw it there, just under the murky surface, undulating, grasping, just *waiting* for me to fall in. Now I looked at it and remembered something from Botany 101, that at least 50 percent of the world's oxygen comes from the ocean. That it's not the rain forest or the entire nation of Canada producing the air we breathe—it's coming from the ocean and the complicated choreography of phytoplankton, grasses, and seaweeds. The gray skin of the ocean and the kelp slithering in the spit of the tide made me shake my head in wonder. What a grand and mysterious world.

At the end of my first day's journey, after wrestling all three bags out of the blue saltshaker of a car, I settled into a B&B, then dined at a little café in Point Reyes Station (population 340). I'd forgotten how fresh, how organic, how totally orgasmic West Coast food can be. Dinner was not long on the plate: an heirloom tomato salad with a mozzarella buratta (a mozzarella ball formed around a soft curd), olive oil, balsamic vinegar, and fresh basil. How could anything so healthful taste so good? Topped off with two excellent glasses of local Sauvignon Blanc recommended by my waitress, I was chattier than usual.

"Are you visiting San Francisco?" the waitress asked.

"No," I answered, "I'm here to see the tule elk in rut. This is the season, yes?"

She frowned. "It's the right time, but with so many tourists trying to catch a glimpse, it's almost impossible. They're spooked by noise."

I must have looked disappointed. "Well," she said, smiling, sliding the check toward me on the table, "try getting an early start. Maybe you'll get lucky."

The restaurant was full of couples plumbing various depths of conversation; some quiet and romantic, others animated and charged. One man stabbed at the air with his fork, apparently feeling the need to drive his point into the atmosphere. Eyes closed, all the sounds swirled around me: Silverware scraping against plates, glasses clinking, kitchen grill sizzling, laughter, coughing, a dog barking somewhere in the distance. It was both oddly comforting and strangely depressing. I was the only single diner in the restaurant. *Surely,* I thought, *this is not loneliness I'm feeling.*

Over the course of nine years I'd traveled all over the place, alone, and never once wished for a companion. What was this emotion tugging at me, asking to be noticed? *OK,* I thought, *just a little more time and "real" life will fade away.* It's one of the things I'd come to love about traveling alone and where it leads—to that moment when the claustrophobia of obligations, worries, and the excess baggage we all carry succumbs to the wide-open space of peace and harmony. There, in that pause of quiet I knew would come at last, I'd have time to figure out what was bothering me.

Back in my room I planned for the next day. The bed-and-breakfast proprietor had told me the same thing the waitress had—that visitors hadn't had much success with tule elk viewings. Too much noise, too many people. *But maybe you'll get lucky!*

I WAS UP EARLY and on the road to Tomales Point before full daylight. The dense fog was not encouraging; it felt like driving through a tunnel stuffed with cotton balls. Mine was the only car on the road. Rabbits and partridges and deer darted in front of or ran alongside me, clearly possessed by some sort of death wish. I rolled along, barely able to see three feet ahead.

At the trailhead, rain began to fall. I hadn't brought the right gear but started anyway, first exploring the historic dairy farm and its abandoned buildings—a feature of the Tomales Point hike. Pierce Point Ranch was built in the 1860s and became the most successful "butter ranch" in the area. It passed through a number of owners and lessees until it ceased operations in 1973. It's now considered by the U.S. National Park Service to be the best example of a 19th-century west Marin County dairy farm, but in the fog it looked decrepit and ominous.

Eleven or so white buildings with gray roofs dotted the fenced-in, flat, and relatively small area. I meandered along a well-worn path, past the main house, the tiny school, and the creamery. There was a slaughterhouse, too, and a blacksmith shop. Old structures no longer in use seem macabre to me, almost menacing. Their implacable stillness seems to say, *The people who were here are long gone, and soon you will be too.* It's as if the windows and doors are eyes and mouths—silent witnesses to the stories and secrets of the people who once lived behind them. In the fog, the whole place looked threatening. I wished again, for a moment, that I wasn't heading out on this hike alone.

One of the old buildings had windows so badly smudged it was as if the room inside were filled with the same fog that was encircling me. Cupping my face against a dirty pane, I strained to see inside and saw what looked like old photographs strewn across the floor. *Strange,* I thought, placing the camera lens against the glass and taking a picture; maybe the camera could "see" better than I could. The digital image made me gasp. Yellowing newspapers and sepia photographs were indeed covering the floor, but next to them was the wispy, white outline of a human shape, male, tall, just standing there. A ghost.

I sincerely hoped this was a figment of my overactive imagination, but there was no denying the "vibe" was disturbing. I wasn't going to spend one more second trying to decide whether the thing inside the building was a phantom or just a photographic anomaly. I was spooked. *Get out of here,* I told myself, making a beeline for the gigantic hay barn. Huge double doors led into the barn at one end, and out onto the trail at the other. I quickly noted the lattice of thick wooden beams overhead, designed to support the weight of a whole winter's worth of hay. Over my shoulder, I snatched one last, nervous look at the ranch just as it was swallowed up by fog.

At the trailhead I read a warning about mountain lions, but there was so little visibility that a sighting would be impossible. I wouldn't see the mountain lion before it saw me, that was for sure. The rain came and went, and so did the mist—it would wrap itself around me like gauze, dissolve to let in the tiniest bit of light, then bear down again. The two-foot-wide dirt path beneath my feet and the tufts of the bushes flanking the trail were the only things I could see. An occasional purple thistle flower offered a brush of color in an otherwise monochromatic palette of gray and white. If I breathed deeply, the air literally dripped into my lungs. Along the way—nine and a half miles round-trip—the surf pounded against the cliffs on either side of the point, though I could barely see the water.

Tomales Point is pummeled on three sides by the Pacific Ocean. Waves crash against the rocky shoreline in a relentless bid to overtake the land. There is nowhere on Tomales Point that you don't hear the waves, even if you can't see them. During that walk I began to think about faith—belief in knowing that what we cannot see is actually there. My blindness while walking required faith in my ears and nose to tell me when I was getting closer to or farther away from the water. On this solitary walk, the clutch of day-to-day worries loosened its grip and eventually fell away on the trail behind me. I love this moment of letting go, so empty of everything yet full of possibility. The gift of solitude was about to be unwrapped on the trail ahead.

I thought about what grounds us when we can't see with our own eyes the things we somehow know are all around us. It goes beyond religious faith: there's something else; a recognition, no matter how indistinct, that we live in the midst of and are part of a million invisible miracles. The simple act of breathing, for instance. We take it for granted because we do it thousands of times a day, every day, until we die. Billions of in and out breaths, and we pause to think about the air only when it's smoky or cold or it's carrying some beautiful scent or curious odor. Yet our ability to breathe air at all depends on plant photosynthesis and the oxygen it releases, a process so profoundly complicated and dense with alchemic mystery whose wonder does not diminish even as the puny human brain attempts to deconstruct it. It's one of those unseen miracles that takes place even in the grass we mow and the weeds we pull. Our very lives depend on it, yet when it's right in front of us, it proceeds undetected and underappreciated. What other miracles abound that we haven't fathomed?

A lyrical, solitary birdsong jolted me out of my reverie. On a knife-blade stump, a tiny wren jumped in place three times, trilling her little heart out to whatever or whomever might be listening in the mist. She seemed completely unaffected by my presence, so I watched until she abruptly took wing and shot out of sight, as fast as a bullet. With visibility limited to the next footstep, I began to notice mundane things like tufts of grass, pinecones, and rocks, because they were the only things I could see. There were enigmatic, tiny tracks on the trail, each one no bigger than a grain of rice. The tracks emerged from the grassy clumps on either side of the trail, made their way to the center of the path, then looped around and went back. A baby snake, maybe? A beetle? And why did the path always revert to its origin? I couldn't even guess at what creature had made such an odd journey.

Woven between tall spikes of grass were spiderwebs, transformed by the dew into jeweled wonders. They were everywhere. I found six unique constructions, all bearing the weight of hundreds of droplets, sparkling like elaborate diamond necklaces strewn about the trail. I slowed way down, purposely searching for them, mesmerized by their excruciating beauty. Suddenly I was seeing spiderweb ornaments everywhere. They were as different from each other as snowflakes, and just as miraculous. Spiders had made webs inside thistle flowers too, silk strands wrapped around the purple blooms like spun sugar, sparkling with tiny droplets.

As I was inspecting a particularly interesting web display, one that looked like a diminutive hammock, some small movement on the ground caught my eye. There it was, the mysterious trackmaker. Kneeling down on the path, I watched as a tiny snail, no bigger than a baby's fingernail, made its slow and deliberate way to the center of the trail. Once there, it stopped, and if you can imagine this, wiggled its minuscule antennae, looked around, then began its purposeful way back. It took quite a long time, but I couldn't take my eyes off it. *Transfixed by a snail,* I thought, *that's a first.* A glance at my watch revealed I'd been out for an hour, yet walked only ten yards. I'd fallen down a rabbit hole and never wanted to leave. It occurred to me briefly that all these enchantments would have gone unnoticed if I'd been distracted by a hiking companion.

Eventually, I forced myself to keep walking, and the sudden movement spooked a flock of birds foraging in the grass and bushes next to me. Hundreds of them burst out of hiding all at once; the powerful drumming of their wings, like the very heart of Nature, seemed to beat in my own chest.

After a while the tightly bunched bushes gave way to open plain where the vegetation huddled close to the ground, and the waves against the rocks sounded farther away and more like gunshots. There were no more spiderwebs or thistles or birds, just the dull sand on the path ahead. The fog would dissipate a little, offering glimpses of small crescents of whitecaps in the distance. Then the mist would press in again so hard I could see it swirling around my ankles like the tide. Even if the tule elk were here it would be impossible to see them through this pall.

I was still thinking—much later—about those spiderwebs, wondering how something so ordinary could become so utterly poetic, when I noticed that I was no longer on the trail. Under my feet was not a sandy path but brown grass that looked completely exhausted. I stopped for a moment in the silence, listening.

The ocean banging on the rocks. Seagulls shrilling overhead. But now I *felt* something too, something different, and it was near me.

Whatever it was, it was big.

The mountain lion warning buzzed in my head, pushing my pulse into chaos.

Fog pressed in again, as white as a blizzard, so I stopped and waited. In the deep silence, punctuated only by the booming of the waves, some large thing moved. I braced myself. There was nowhere to run but into oblivion.

But then, as it had all throughout my walk, the fog began to dissolve and out of the mist 30 feet in front of me, the outline of a bull elk appeared. First his enormous antlers, then his head, the chocolate brown of his mane. He blinked his wet, brown eyes at me, so close I could see his lashes. Appearing and disappearing in the fog like this, he looked like some mythical creature, a preternatural vision, an animal spirit.

Was I really seeing this? The bull and I looked at each other while shadows stirred all around me, and I suddenly realized I was in the middle of an enormous elk herd. There were *dozens* of them, grazing, ambling. And the big bull stood there, never taking his eyes off me.

I stood in the middle of the tule elks for a long time while they ate grass, squabbled with each other, trotted away from or toward something compelling. Some of the cows brushed by me as if I were nonexistent. I suppose it's possible they didn't see me, but the bull did. My heart pounded not from fear but from the recognition I'd slipped into some magical place, where animal and human were not enemies but living creatures sharing the same air and standing on the same ground. In this breathless moment, so unlike anything else I'd ever felt, I wondered if I had died: seeing the ghostly apparition back at the ranch; the elk cows acting as if I were invisible; my super-heightened state of perception; these were all so strange and defied easy explanation. My solitude had delivered to me a moment of grace, a secret glimpse into what it means and how it feels to be completely connected to life and everything in it. Far from being dead, this, I realized, was how it's supposed to feel to be alive.

The bull finally and slowly nodded his noble head toward me, as if to say, *Go on now*. The fog had completely dissipated. Reluctantly, I turned and left them, walking out of and away from the trance that had for more than an hour completely mesmerized me.

The trail from which I'd strayed wasn't far. Away from the bull and his harem, I looked around—in the full brightness of day, there was the ocean, here was the meadow, the sky, the sun, and the sandy path I'd walked in on. It all seemed so ordinary now, the extraordinary moment forever passed.

Far away, back down the path, human voices announced the arrival of hikers. I watched from a distance as the bull led his harem away toward silence. The noisy group approaching would never know that the very thing they were seeking had been massed before them just moments ago. As much as I'd wished at the beginning of the hike for a companion, it was exactly *because* I was alone that I'd stumbled upon the elk. If I'd been talking, whistling, or even walking with purpose, the elk would have heard me and been long gone.

The hike to the end of Tomales Point took hours. Along the way I noticed other elk herds in distant meadows, napping in the sun. Most of the land was barren, but random clumps of scrubby bushes offered shelter for birds, lizards, and coyotes. In a stand of cypress trees, I heard an owl hooting in broad daylight. A heron flew soundlessly overhead. It was peaceful and lovely, but now that I could see everything, it was almost as if I was incapable of noticing anything but the obvious.

At the end of Tomales Point, steep, unfenced bluffs dropped sharply to the desolate beaches below. By the time I reached the point itself and sat on the edge of a thousand-foot cliff to eat my lunch, the sun had burned off every vestige of the mist. Far below, cormorants blackened the jagged, mottled sea rocks, and the only person for miles around was a lone diver bobbing next to his boat, anchored a few hundred feet offshore. The whole thing felt terribly lonely yet completely connected.

My definition of "lonely" had been challenged today. Yes, I was by myself and I'd be going back to a hotel room alone, but I'd stumbled into a series of moments that were astonishing, as if I'd been granted a glimpse through a secret window. It was an affirmation that no matter how strongly we cling to the notion that it's people who make us feel connected, that isn't where the truth lies. When I saw the webs, felt the birds, looked into the eye of a tule elk, an internal gear clicked into place and began ticking me along a different path. Solitude isn't about being alone, it's about being receptive to the energies all around, and once touched by them, I was linked in a way that felt elemental and essential. And rare. Those energies immersed me wholly in the moment; they made feel deeply alive. Happiness, I knew then, was never going to come in the form of "another." It would come to me in fits and starts all throughout my life's journey, as long as I took time to notice it.

At the end of those nine and a half miles, my feet were so sore I wanted to lie down on the trail and wait for a Girl Scout troop with a gurney to carry me to my car. Eventually, I limped past the spot where, hours before, I'd been enchanted by dew-laden webs. In the dazzling light of day, they were no longer visible, at least to me. How many beautiful details in everyday life have I failed to notice, I wondered, because I was too busy looking for something—or someone—else?

Nature, I now realized, had to make me blind so I could see her. The fog had walled me in. There was no forward, no retreat, just here where I'd stood. The whole time I'd been caught in a web of past memories, even as the present moment was leading me to exactly what I'd come to see.

I knew two things then: I'd never have the experience of the jeweled spiderwebs and the tule elk again, and it would never have happened if I'd not been alone.

All the miseries of mankind come from one thing, not knowing how to remain alone. —Blaise Pascal

TWENTY THOUSAND MILES of uncertainty stretched ahead of him; a long, lonely road that 25-year-old Dominic Gill would pedal, taking more than two years of his life to do it. Months earlier, back in Oldham, England, the idea had seemed so tantalizing: ride a tandem bicycle from the tip of Alaska to the tip of South America and make a documentary film about it. Along the way, invite others to pedal along on the backseat. Pass through countries and learn about their cultures and their customs, and make new friends. But as he headed out of Deadhorse, Alaska, on June 16, 2006, with only four days' worth of meager food rations, the idea no longer seemed exciting but daunting and depressing. Loneliness hadn't yet laid its cold hand upon him, but he could feel it waiting for him in the stark and featureless landscape ahead.

Two years, one month, and twenty-two days later, Dominic and a companion pedaled the last 20 miles of the journey, arriving at the southern tip of the Western Hemisphere. More than 270 buddies had helped Dom complete his epic journey; countless others had cheered and supported him, fed him, and given him faith in the inherent goodness of people.

To say Dom's story is inspiring is to gloss over the pain and suffering and danger he endured. It was a hard two-plus years. The difficulties began even before he left England. His own father tried to talk him out of it. His northern Canadian girlfriend left him. On the plane approaching Alaska, Dom almost talked himself out of it, too. Secretly, he hoped that the three separate shipping containers holding his tandem bike had lost each other in transit. Then he could back out and not lose face. But at the baggage claim, there they were—three bike boxes, carefully stacked and undamaged. What spurred him over that final obstacle of doubt was the worry that if he didn't proceed as planned, he would end up living a life of regret.

I first met Dom at the Banff Mountain Film Festival and World Tour screening of his film, *Take a Seat*. In the film and in person, Dominic's confidence and candor are impressive, and I was interested in hearing what he had to say about solitude. Two-plus years on the road is a long time, and given the terrain he traveled (Alaska, all of northwestern Canada, the United States, and sparsely inhabited regions of Mexico and Central and South America), there would have to have been days, if not weeks, of inescapable solitude.

There were, and those periods of alone time were painful for Dom. When he began the trip, already full of misgivings about the undertaking, he was still hurting from the breakup with his girlfriend. Early on, in northwestern Canada, he endured a week where he had no meaningful interaction with people, where the enormous blanket of tundra and stunted spruce forest reminded him, moment by moment, of the heartbreak he was trying to escape. He likened the external landscape to his internal one, a series of "peaks and troughs" that would alternately—over the two-year journey—take him from extreme happiness to extreme sadness. Later in the trip, when Dom settled into a community for a period of time, developing fast but compelling friendships, it would become more and more difficult to pull away, to face what he knew would be a "massively intense loneliness," as he left this stopping point to pedal to the next.

Dom viewed solitude as a "necessary evil," a bridge spanning the friends he left behind and the new ones he was about to make. It was in those periods of solitude that Dom experienced his deepest "troughs," so it was no wonder he dreaded time alone. Yet he admits that his best and most cohesive ideas emerged as he came out of the "tail end of one of those deep troughs . . . sadness is a much more powerful trigger for me than happiness."

When Dom settled into a new place for a while, he would sometimes think that this was the place he could live, these were the people who could become his new friends, and that he could be happy there. He says the heartbreak and his aversion to loneliness had made him "way more clingy, mentally" and vulnerable to the seduction of human attention. But Dom knew that on some level he was succumbing to a kind of weakness, and so, without exception, at some point in his pseudo settling-in period, he'd feel a "trigger" go off and within no time be back on the road again, pedaling through the loneliness he despised. Solitude, however much Dom hated it, kept leading him, over and over again, to strength.

Solitude, Dom told me, became a conduit between one grand experience and the next. It helped him gain perspective on the importance of human relationships, and it made him appreciate them even more when they were suddenly left behind on a ribbon of road that seemed to have no end. Those dark moments of loneliness gave Dominic time to explore his mind, arriving at conclusions that might have eluded him otherwise. Transience, he realized, was like a drug to him; it was the "easiest way to keep feeding on the new." At the end of the trip, Dom recognized a shift in his thinking. "The ultimate dream for me," he said, "would be to be able to be so absorbent and observant that I could find new things and make the most of every single day in the same place."

Solitude led Dom to epiphanies he hadn't been seeking, just as at Tomales Point it had led me to feel more connected to life than I'd thought possible.

CULTURALLY, SOLITUDE IS FRAMED in profoundly different ways. In mainstream North America, solitude is seen as privation: we use solitary confinement, time out, and social banishment as ways to exert punishment. For a long time, the worst fate a woman could face was to be older and single. A spinster. That perception has changed somewhat, but not entirely. Many people I've known—women and men—would rather have dental work performed on them sans anesthetic than be seen alone at dinner or a movie. "I don't want anyone feeling sorry for me," they say. Solitude appears for many to be synonymous with loneliness or worse—pathos—but it's neither. Intentional solitude allows a release from the "noise" of others in order to think about things, connect with nature, or just be still. We're not taught by North American society to value solitude, nor are we encouraged to build it into our daily lives. But it is, ironically, the very thing—perhaps the only thing—that allows us to begin the process of personal and spiritual fulfillment.

When I first started traveling alone, everyone thought I was crazy. *Why wouldn't you want to take someone along,* they asked, *and isn't it lonely to be out there all by yourself?* After more than a decade of traveling alone I now realize that solitude doesn't create loneliness, it simply reveals it. Eliminate distractions, give yourself enough time to think things through, and your inner landscape becomes clearer. If you feel lonely, it's not because you are alone. It's because something else is missing in your life, and it might not be a person; it could simply be the lack of solitude, the time needed to get to know yourself. On my many forays into the woods, whether on a trip somewhere or hiking at home, it takes only about 30 minutes before a sense of harmony and connectedness becomes palpable. This happens without fail, yet I'm always surprised when it does. In choosing to be linked to chaos—particularly our self-imposed slavery to technology—we've unintentionally disconnected ourselves from a natural source of solitude, peace, and balance. Spending any substantial time alone in nature will fill us up, and it's so easy to do, really. Yet we place so many layers between ourselves and nature that it's no wonder we soon forget to live *in* it instead of around it.

On any given day, consider how many layers we construct. There's the door itself, to shield us from the heat, the cold, the bugs, the perceived danger. When we're behind the door, we lose our vital and essential connection to the very thing that sustains us—Earth. We lose our adaptability to cold, to heat, to sun, to rain. Separation from the natural world creates a physiological stasis that is essentially unnatural and is based on disconnection. We feel it as a hunger, a longing, but we fail to recognize for what it is, so we seek ways to feed it—through food, sex, tangible objects, work. Yet all those things add more layers and increase the distance between us and our corporeal connection to the energy of life.

Feeling that connection every day for a week or two is precisely the reason I travel alone, and I've also had to build it into my life at home, to bridge the gaps between one trip and the next. This "quiet time" has to be planned well in advance, and once it's on my schedule, it cannot be interfered with, whether it's an hour or two or a full day. Quiet time includes a vow of silence—incoming and outgoing—(barring elements out of one's control). No radio, iPod, television, or talking. No clatter that can be avoided. Phones get turned off or unplugged. On my quiet days, I'm up early in the morning, before the wildlife have gone into hiding, and I take a long hike or horseback ride through the woods to get me centered right away.

There is so much to hear when you shut out the extraneous noise of your own talking: how wind in the leaves sounds like a rushing stream; how a squirrel running through dead leaves sounds as big as a bear; a hundred different birdsongs; how forest air smells different in the rain than it does in the sun. Details are everywhere, and on a "quiet day" I have nowhere to be and no one else to please, so I'm free to take as much time as I want to notice minutiae. Depending on the season, I may do something outside after dark. If it's summer, I hope for a thunderstorm so I can sit on the porch and watch the flash of lightning as it tears up the sky, and stare into the rain as it blows sideways in thick, billowy water curtains.

On fall evenings, I might make a small fire outside, feed it till it's blazing, then watch the process of it consuming itself, the color of the flame changing from bright orange to a white-hot blue. Sometimes I'll just sit in a rocking chair on the porch in the dark, thinking. And my favorite thing is setting up a place to sleep outside and waking up to the dawn. No need for an alarm. Outside the door, everything comes alive when the sun wakes up the world.

Water, fire, air. All free. All right outside our doors, just a single intention away. If not for a day, then for an hour.

We don't stack up layers just between us and nature; we do the same thing to our psyches. Sogyal Rinpoche, a Tibetan Dzogchen lama and author of *The Tibetan Book of Living and Dying*, points out that we are "cramming our lives with compulsive activity so that there is no time at all to confront the real issues." Inside each of us is the seed of our potential—or think of it as the fundamental taproot of who and what we are. Unintentionally or not, we rarely give it the space, the nourishment, or the light it needs to blossom into self-knowledge. We heap layer after layer on top of it—distractions, obsessions, commitments—so that it stays buried within us, patiently waiting in the dark. When we finally expose it to light, it can begin to grow at last, unhindered. That's when we really start to live.

One story that illustrates the notion of solitude creating the fertile ground for revelation is that of Japan's venerated poet Matsuo Basho. Born about 1644 in feudal Japan to a samurai father, Basho began studying poetry at a young age and quickly became recognized for his talent. Eventually, he moved to Edo, what is now Tokyo, where he became a noted haiku master. Despite, or maybe because of, the fame that brought him many relationships, students, and admirers, Basho seems to have suffered a spiritual and emotional crisis in his mid-40s. "I feel lonely as I gaze at the moon, I feel lonely as I think about myself, and I feel lonely as I ponder upon this wretched life of mine. I want to cry out that I am lonely, but no one asks me how I feel." And what was his antidote to this crisis? Seeking more solitude.

His despair led him to take long journeys, sometimes covering hundreds of miles, mostly on foot, and mostly alone, or with only one other companion. Basho needed time to think deeply about the essence of nature and man's place in it. He used solitude to forge an ever stronger connection to the natural world, which filled him with wonder, awe, and peace. On one of his long travels through the Yoshino Mountains, Basho—the inveterate wordsmith—gazed upon a waving sea of cherry trees in blossom and was so overcome by their beauty he could not write. Solitude, for Basho, helped him defeat his sense of loneliness by revealing the truth of man and nature as one shared form of energy, the same epiphany I had at Point Reyes as I gazed in wonder at the elk.

For the remainder of his life, Basho continued to take long, contemplative trips. The one he made in 1689, a 1,200-mile journey on foot through northern Japan, resulted in his classic *Oku no Hosomichi—Narrow Road to a Far Province.*

A year before he died, still revered as a poet and sought by many, Basho took to bolting his garden gate in order to protect the solitude he now knew was his spiritual solace. Ironically, he had shifted away from expecting people to cure his loneliness and instead understood that it was in solitude that he would find the connection he sought.

Traversing the mountains and fields of Japan, over many years and thousands of miles, Basho stripped away the layers that separated him from both nature and his own poetry, and, exposed again to the light, his creativity grew like a tree toward the sun, its branches still reaching us today.

Solitude is a precious commodity and its value should not be underestimated. John Muir and Everett Ruess, vastly different personalities, both decided to shed the heavy cloak of frenzied civilization and set out alone into the wilderness to find peace, beauty, and answers.

Born in 1838 in Scotland, John Muir came to America with his family when he was 11. Much of his boyhood was spent on three things: fighting in the schoolyard; searching for bird nests; and, under the constant threat of a lashing by his father, learning by heart the entire New and Old Testaments of the Bible. Muir's affinity for the natural world may have begun as a reaction to his strict religious upbringing, but it was never a frivolous attraction.

When Muir enrolled in college, he discovered the science of botany and, like me, fell down his own rabbit hole. He would run with wild enthusiasm into the fields for his botany lessons, eliciting smiles, chuckles, and head shakes from his fellow students. His classmates may have found his passion amusing, but no one doubted Muir's sincerity.

Despite his cynicism toward organized religion, Muir was deeply spiritual, believing that God was present in every leaf, every raindrop, in the scales of river trout, the fringed leaves of cypress trees. After an industrial accident damaged one of his eyes, Muir spent six miserable weeks in darkened rooms, emerging from the trauma determined to follow nature wherever she led him. "This affliction has driven me to the sweet fields. God has to nearly kill us sometimes to teach us lessons."

In September 1867, Muir began a journey by foot of nearly a thousand miles, from Indiana to Florida. Once there, he decided to hop a ship to South America to continue his wanderings, but a case of malaria contracted along Florida's Gulf Coast changed his plans and the course of U.S. history. Instead of disembarking in South America, Muir made his way to northern California. He immediately set out for a weeklong visit to Yosemite, a place he'd not seen but had heard plenty about. He was transfixed by its grandeur: "No temple made with hands can compare with Yosemite," he said. He built a cabin in the woods in Yosemite Valley, constructing it so that one corner of the small structure allowed nearby Yosemite Creek to flow freely beneath it. Plants sprouted up through the cabin floorboards, and Muir's writing desk was overhung by an arch of ferns whose tendrils he had woven together. Below the floorboards, grass grew, frogs peeped, and water babbled. Muir gained comfort and clarity from the sounds of nature beneath his feet: "Every particle of rock or water or air has God by its side leading it the way it should go. . . . In God's wildness lies the hope of the world."

From the cabin, Muir would travel alone into the backcountry carrying little: a tin cup, some tea, bread, and a volume of Emerson, whose writings deeply resonated with him. Over time, Muir led many people on guided forays into the woods and mountains—including Emerson himself and President Theodore "Teddy" Roosevelt—but he preferred to wander by himself: "Only by going alone in silence, without baggage, can one truly get into the heart of the wilderness. All other travel is mere dust and hotels and baggage and chatter."

As he aged, Muir charmed the public with his rhapsodic language and Scottish lilt. His love affair with nature could have been easily dismissed as quirky or kooky—the ramblings of a hermit—but he exuded such earnestness and authenticity when he spoke or wrote of it that there was no denying he was onto something real. "Take a course in good water and air; and in the eternal youth of Nature you may renew your own. Go quietly, alone; no harm will befall you," he encouraged. "The clearest way into the Universe is through a forest wilderness."

Solitude created a venue for the advancement of Muir's unity with nature, leading him to worship the natural world in a way most people worship their God. His solitary wanderings in northern California refreshed him but also led him to the conclusion and conviction that places like Yosemite needed permanent protection from exploitation

In 1903, the President came to Yosemite and met with Muir. At this point in his life, Muir had founded the Sierra Club and was gravely concerned about the state of California's mismanagement and exploitation of Yosemite. Roosevelt and Muir talked incessantly about the wild world, and at Roosevelt's suggestion, they left the presidential escort behind in order to go deep into the backcountry and set up camp by themselves. One can only guess how Roosevelt reacted to Muir's ecstatic proclamations and ringing praise for the mountains and the rivers and the connectedness of all things. "God has cared for these trees, saved them from drought, disease, avalanches, and a thousand tempests and floods. But he cannot save them from fools." By the time the men emerged from the wilderness, Roosevelt shared Muir's vision. Yosemite would have federal protection.

Without John Muir, we might well not have the grand and exceptional National Park System we have today, not to mention the Sierra Club and numerous other movements dedicated to preserving forests and rivers. The entire world has reaped the benefit of Muir's time spent in solitude. Certainly, I wouldn't have been able to walk the length of Tomales Point amid herds of wild elk if it weren't for Muir's influence. That prime piece of real estate would have long ago been snapped up and "developed" if protections weren't in place.

"Thousands of tired, nerve-shaken, over-civilized people are beginning to find out . . . that wilderness is a necessity; and that mountain parks and reservations are useful not only as fountains of timber and irrigating rivers, but as fountains of life," he wrote. And, as he famously proclaimed, "Climb the mountains and get their good tidings. Nature's peace will flow into you as sunshine flows into trees. The winds will blow their own freshness into you, and the storms their energy, while cares will drop off like autumn leaves."

Far less well known than Muir, Everett Ruess was born into a wealthy southern California family in 1914. But early in life, he became disillusioned by the culture he found himself in, filled, he felt, with materialism, greed, and vapidity. At the age of 15, when most boys are thinking about *female* natural wonders, he wrote a poem called "Pledge to the Wind":

By the strength of my arm, by the sight of my eyes
By the skill of my fingers, I swear,
As long as life dwells in me, never will I
Follow any way but the sweeping way of the wind.

He felt such a strong need to get away that he embraced an extreme form of solitude, leaving behind his friends, family, and worldly possessions to discover himself in the wilderness of the American Southwest.

Ruess was a light-haired, slender, somewhat androgynous-looking 20-year-old artist and adventurer known for his simple and vivid Japanese-like woodcuts and paintings when he set out in 1934 for what would be his last wandering into the wild. Riding into town on a burro, legs dangling almost to the ground and pulling behind him two overpacked mules, he must have been quite a sight to the residents, who were accustomed to seeing nothing on the horizon but the sun in the morning. Alone with his animals in the labyrinth of the backcountry, Ruess thought about life, the state of humanity, and his own purpose. His writings reveal a depth of reflection unusual for someone so young but perhaps not so surprising given the extraordinary amount of time he spent alone in the solitude of nature. One letter home proclaimed, "I have seen almost more beauty than I can bear"—reminiscent of Basho's encounter with the cherry blossoms.

Ruess had not been so much seduced by nature as abducted by her. "I prefer the saddle to the streetcar and star-sprinkled sky to a roof, the obscure and difficult trail, leading into the unknown, to any paved highway, and the deep peace of the wild to the discontent bred by cities . . . it is enough that I am surrounded by beauty."

One of Ruess's happiest journeys was hiking the John Muir Trail, which begins in Yosemite National Park and continues 215 miles through the Ansel Adams Wilderness, Sequoia National Park, and Kings Canyon National Park, ending at the highest peak in the continental United States, 14,496-foot Mount Whitney.

Despite his youth, Ruess became friends with, and was admired by, the photographers Ansel Adams and Dorothea Lange. Adams and Lange were mature artists, secure in their craft, so it's noteworthy that they recognized the depth of Ruess's love affair with nature.

He didn't always have an easy time of it, though, having to endure the difficulties inherent in living a vagabond life, eking out a meager living off the land. But Ruess stuck fast to the pledge he'd made to the wind, the promise to only and always follow nature to where she would lead him. "Say that I starved, that I was lost and weary, that I was burned and blinded by the desert sun, footsore, thirsty, sick with strange diseases, lonely and wet and cold, but that I kept my dream!"

Ruess was 20 when he disappeared, and that disappearance has become the stuff of legend, a mystery never definitively solved. Ironically, his death, far from being a deterrent to those romantic souls who long to shed the bit and bridle of daily life, has become an inspiration, an invitation to run free, in beauty.

Ruess had spent most of his young adulthood alone, yet one thing is clear from his letters: he loved his life and his choice to spend it among the cliffs and the ravens and under the bright white stars. For him, death was not a tragedy, but dying anywhere except in his beloved wilderness would have been. In nature he felt whole, peaceful, and unjudged. "While I am alive, I intend to live. . . . I have not tired of the wilderness; rather I enjoy its beauty and the vagrant life I lead, more keenly all the time. . . . Always I shall be one who loves the wilderness: Swaggers and softly creeps between the mountain peaks; I shall listen long to the sea's brave music; I shall sing my song above the shriek of desert winds." His woodcut prints of trees, rock formations, and rivers communicate an affinity with his subjects that is completely without pretense or self-consciousness. Like Muir, Ruess not only "got it," he lived it. Both men achieved, through their solitary wanderings, a kind of symbiosis with nature that the rest of us can only yearn for.

While mainstream America eschews solitude, other cultures so appreciate its potential that they use it as an intentional tool for self-discovery. Traditionally, among many Native Americans, the critical turning point in a young person's life was marked by a "vision quest," an intensely personal and solitary journey into the wilderness to discover the vision or dream that would influence one's future direction in life.

Because a person had to be physically and psychologically ready to receive a vision, the quest was not entered into haphazardly. It was a solemn ritual, requiring three critical components. The first was preparation. Questers would spend days, weeks, or months, preparing for their quest; the final arrangements included cleansing the body and fasting.

The second component was the quest itself. The solo journey into the wilderness was meant to beckon, with humility and wonder, the vision. The seeker was not to return to the community until her or his true spiritual name and life's path had been revealed.

The third component was the concept of obligation. The seeker *must* come back and live out her or his destiny as revealed during the vision quest. So while it was an intensely personal pilgrimage, it was also a way to strengthen and bind communities. The value of solitude was communally recognized because it ultimately benefited everyone.

Within Plains Indian cultures, vision quests often took place in thunderstorm season so that questers would have to witness and coexist with the natural world in all its fearsome power. Vision seekers, usually adolescents, endured cold, hunger, predation, and isolation until in some form their true name and future was revealed to them. Visions were messages from the Great Spirit, considered a gift, and once enlightened, the seeker was obligated to come back to the community and to live out the vocation that had been revealed.

A number of young Native Americans today still embark on vision quests. Imagine what it's like, striding out into the wild, with no food, no water, and no one to come to your rescue. You find your spot, dig a pit, and stay there for three or four days until something happens. The sense of isolation must be profound. The sense of some grand thing about to happen must be visceral. But the logistics of it must be horrible: lying in a dirt pit, perhaps in a thunderstorm, in the deep night, cold, hungry, alone, waiting for the kindness of the universe to deliver unto you a message. If you hadn't taken the quest seriously going in, it wouldn't be long before you gave it your full attention.

Today, the value of the vision quest has been resurrected and is used not only by Native American communities but by mainstream religions and leadership development programs. Google "personal vision quest" and you will find dozens of these programs scattered all over North America, from the Southwest deserts to the Vermont mountains. These programs require a commitment of at least a few days to as many as ten days spent alone in the wilderness. Though it may sound difficult and lonely, these programs are growing in popularity, and not because they're an easy fix or because they offer a quick way to enlightenment. People are realizing that in order to find themselves, they first must commit to getting lost for a while, to spending unaccustomed time alone, and, frankly, to suffering.

In this context, solitude is used intentionally to help people find an authentic connection to their spirituality, their communities, and themselves. In order to do that, the person must be separated from every distraction that threatens to cloud the vision or the epiphany. When people are taken out of their comfort zones and left to fend for themselves, wondrous things happen. Ironically, the biggest challenge most folks face in undertaking the quest is not the hunger, the cost, or the cold, or even the fear. It's the anxiety of being alone.

It was my solo travels that convinced me of the necessity of creating space for alone time. Between my trips, sometimes as much as a year would go by and the opportunities for real, extended solitude were few. My structured "quiet times" were nice, but I couldn't always devote that much time to solitude. As a way to be alone, I also took walks through the neighborhood at night, when most people with sense were already tucked into bed. Or I'd get to work early and sit in the car for 15 minutes. Something I started years ago but still haven't mastered is to sit out on my porch at dusk and listen while each species of bird stops singing. Which stops first? Which stops last? They appear to stop in order of species, then there's a brief but clear demarcation between when the birds fall silent and the frogs' communal chorus begins. My concentration on this bird riddle lasts maybe 15 minutes at the most, and then I am suddenly somewhere else in my mind. By the time I realize the critical moment has once again eluded me, I'm deep in other thoughts. The payoff is that I leave refreshed and ready for what's next.

Solitude, when used in the framework of this book, is not meant to isolate you from the world. You can make solitude for yourself anytime, anywhere, incorporating it into your daily life. It's a way to get out of the incessant whirring machine of living and into a quiet, contemplative place. In solitude, you will begin to calm your mind and notice the details of your own state of being, and of the world around you. Both are important, because if you can't be still, you won't be able to recognize quiet clues when they begin to surface. These clues will help you find a way to open the door to a deeper understanding of yourself and a new way to see the world. Solitude is the gift of an unfettered and undistracted period of time to go into the next phase, which is introspection. True, meaningful introspection can happen only in solitude, when the mind is free from distractions.

There are two kinds of solitude—the kind you fill up with junk and noise while you're cleaning the house or driving to work, and the other kind, where you carve out 15 minutes, an hour, or a day of alone time to think deeply about things that matter, problems that need solving, decisions that need to be made by choice, not by default. Your life's path.

Used purposefully, solitude naturally includes an element of silence, and silence, like solitude, is a rare commodity—yet so valuable in the process of growth. Emily Hsu, a teacher with the Tse Chen Ling Center for Tibetan Buddhist Studies in San Francisco, offers these thoughts on the usefulness of being quiet: "Staying in silence for periods of time is a practice that many practitioners engage in, particularly when they enter a meditation retreat. Many group retreats, both in the Tibetan Buddhist tradition and the Theravada tradition, include silence as a mandatory element of the retreat. Silence enables one to go more deeply into one's practice and increase one's mindfulness and awareness. It also helps one to quiet the mind. Buddhist practice is focused on taming and transforming the mind, and talking often distracts us from being aware.

"Also, many of us tend to mindlessly engage in unconstructive speech and staying in silence for a period of time helps us to be more aware of those habits and enables us to change them in the future."

Emily's point about mindlessly engaging in unconstructive speech rings as clearly as a Tibetan singing bowl. Think about how much talking you are required to do during the day and how much of it has substance. How much of it is insightful, wise? How much of it actually helps make things better? Deliberately being silent, whether for an hour or part of a day, is another way to experience solitude even amid other people. Inviting silence in the middle of the daily bedlam is a really powerful way to calm the commotion of our minds and allow for better concentration. A self-imposed silence, practiced with integrity, allows us to "hear" who we are. Our thoughts, no longer jostled aside or drowned out by the distraction of speech, can reveal to us many things— fears, hopes, dreams, desires. Once revealed, these thoughts can be examined more fully, leading almost always to somewhere else: to a plan, some new resolve, or just an understanding of why something is the way it is. The knowledge that comes from solitude and introspection creates a more self-aware, insightful person, who can handle pressures and bring wisdom to daily decisions at home and in life.

MY FIRST EXPERIENCE with a deliberate vow of silence came unexpectedly on a desert hike I took in Joshua Tree National Park, in southeastern California, a few years after my hike at Point Reyes National Seashore and about eight months after I'd heard rumors of an organizational merger between my Girl Scout council and several others. I was to be there four days before attending a conference in Palm Springs. On the drive in, I began the process of separation by turning off the radio and the cell phone. I knew they'd stay that way for the next four days, even though I hadn't yet considered a deliberate vow of silence.

It was early February in the Mojave Desert, and there was no way I'd be able to sleep under the stars without freezing my arthritic limbs into immovable posts, so I'd rented a cabin at a B&B in Twentynine Palms, a town just outside the park. When I pulled into the dusty dirt driveway, my heart sank. The buildings, scattered haphazardly all over the place, looked deserted. After wandering around the grounds for what seemed like half an hour, I grudgingly turned on the cell phone and called the phone number for the inn. Amanda, the hostess, popped out of one of the many structures and led me out among the cabins. They'd looked so appealing on the Internet. Now they seemed like nothing more than shacks stuck out in the sand. So when she opened the door to my room, I was more than pleasantly surprised to see a charming self-contained living space with an overstuffed bed, sitting room, armoire, kitchen, a very nicely appointed bathroom, good furniture, good art . . . and a resident owl just outside. There used to be two of them, a mated pair, but according to Amanda, the female had just died, probably from d-CON poisoning. The male sat in the yucca tree *hoo-hoo*ing and waiting for his mate to come back. It was such a sad, lonely, extended plea for her return. I wondered how long it would take before various hungers spurred him to abandon his waiting and create a new life.

I spent that night in my cabin, far away from everyone and everything. No television, no noise, and when I thought about going into town to get something to eat, the prospect of opening my mouth and making words was so unappealing I stayed in the room and ate trail mix. What would it be like, I wondered, to be completely silent for a while? If there was ever a place to try it, this was it. Unless completely unavoidable, I told myself, I would not say a word for two days. That was the first of a practice I'd repeat more than once in the years to come.

Joshua Tree National Park is an interesting convergence of two ecosystems—the Mojave and Colorado deserts. Joshua trees (supposedly named by the Mormons after Joshua with his outstretched, beckoning arms), grow only in the Mojave and Sonoran deserts, with a few scattered in the San Bernardino Mountains; cross the Colorado River and they disappear. In so many ways, they are a metaphor for all tender, living things. They rely on others in order to thrive and be beautiful: on the yucca moth, which simultaneously pollinates the plant and lays her eggs in its bloom; on the weather; and on a perfect confluence of environmental conditions. Lacking these, Joshua trees grow straight, with no "arms"—limbs—and while they may look strong and majestic, they are more vulnerable to wind, weather, and disaster. I suppose, like people, the more "arms" they grow, the more adaptable they become.

My first hike was up 5,461-foot Ryan Mountain. I had dressed in many layers, wrapped my head and face in a gator scarf and earmuffs, worn gloves, and *still* the wind shredded me as if I were a paper doll. At several points, even with my face completely covered by fleece, I had to use my hands to shield my ears and cheeks. It was 41°F, but the wind had to be more than 40 miles an hour. The cold seemed not just to find its way in but *attack* its way in. Occasionally there was a respite, and then I would pause in my upward climb to turn around and gaze upon the scenery. Stunning in its vastness: a complete 360 degrees with no sign of habitation except for the road. These unfettered landscapes always make me think of the indigenous people and what it must have been like for them to be sitting atop a mountain or a favorite meditation rock, and see the first wagon train cutting its way across the prairie. Or to be a native collecting coconuts on the beach and witness the first galleon appear on the horizon. Lacking context, I wonder what their visceral reaction was. In any event, whenever I survey a landscape so harsh and challenging, I feel sad that the people who could deal with the land on the land's terms were forced out, replaced by others who wasted no time exploiting it.

The cold was simply not going to abate that day on Ryan Mountain, and even the exertion of climbing the mountain was not warming me sufficiently. I thought about sanctuary and warmth, even just the heater in the rental car, but then realized I wasn't being in the moment. I wasn't present, even though I had promised myself I would take my time. In the desert, that's so important because the magnificent details aren't obvious. The subtleties of the landscape are brilliant but only recognizable if you slow down. Here in the desert, the lush tropical palms, the brilliantly blooming prickly pear cacti, the profusion of purple, gold, red, and orange wildflowers that flash in the sun for a short time and then disappear—all of this life has to endure relentless punishment and agonizing brutality throughout its life cycle. And yet, when their moment comes, it's full of heroic effort.

I knew as a human interloper that as long as I could forgo my own comfort for a while, I could become part of that moment—the moment when the Indian paintbrush opens its flowers to the sun or the yellow blossom on the cactus begins to droop. I could be part of the irony of hiking on a cold, sunny day, and suddenly be in the midst of swirling snowflakes from a storm cloud 30 miles away. I absorbed each step, each visual, aural, and olfactory stimulation and thought, *This is what my life is, right now*. Nothing else mattered.

Out of the side of the mountain grew a twisted, desperate-looking tree that made me think about the piñon pine, how it can be hundreds of years old and only four or five feet high, gnarled and stubby in a way that reveals its toil. It will grow out of a crack in a rock or off the sheer side of a cliff, and despite the unrelenting winds, it pushes, pushes, *pushes* skyward. It simply won't give up. In the United States, you don't see piñon pines anywhere else but the Southwest desert. Maybe they need the drama of the life-or-death struggle. You can tell a lot about the life of a piñon by the direction of its growth, which way it had to strain, and where it could rest. The most ironic ones are those that reach four or five feet, defiant against all odds, and then get zapped by a thunderbolt. Such valorous trees, really. Even after struggling to survive and getting cracked to oblivion in a flash of lightning, the base that's left will eventually begin to grow a new tree.

These trees continue to be a source of inspiration to me—the irresistible thrust of life's will against acquiescence. The life of a piñon pine is all about being sure of the moment. *This is the moment, right now, when the wind has abated and I can stop spending energy struggling—in this moment of calm I can shoot skyward. Now, here, is the moment when the wind is beating me, so I will hunker down and fight it until it relents, and then I will creep forward. And I will keep doing this, every day.*

That night, I dined at Twentynine Palms Inn, interested to see if I could remain mute when asked to speak my dinner order. It wasn't that hard. I smiled at the waitress, pointed to what I wanted on the menu, nodded yes or no when she asked me questions, gave her the thumbs-up when she inquired how everything was. It was pretty simple, and I guess, it being California, they'd seen stranger things. Dinner was a raw vegetable plate, navy bean soup, and salmon with lemon-butter sauce, all accompanied by live acoustic Spanish music. Despite the fact that there was noise everywhere, I still felt the calmness of my own self-imposed silence. It was lovely.

Later, back at the cabin, the lonely widower owl hooted in the tree outside my room. I ventured out with a flashlight and stood beneath him. The porch light, weak though it was, reflected off the owl's breast feathers. Behind him, an ink sky was ripped open by the white, piercing light of a million stars. And on the edge of the desert sand, where the darkness ate the light, coyotes ran back and forth, yipping and howling.

I stood in the cold desert air, at the line between civilization and wild. Listening to those hungry calls, the howling sounding closer and closer, the small hairs on my neck and arms stood on end. I tingled in the way you know is a warning and went inside, for safety. No matter how removed we are from the natural world, no matter how civilized we become, in the night we are still animals, vulnerable and sometimes full of fear.

On my last silent day, I started early to beat the desert heat but also to give myself time to drive back to Palm Springs for the conference. From the parking lot, the hike in to the 49 Palms Oasis trail didn't look like much—a pile of rubble and a steep climb to brown, burned-out patches of scrub. It didn't take long to gain a fair bit of altitude. Down in the parking lot, my car looked like nothing more than a child's toy. It was only 7:30 a.m., but my shirt was already drenched in sweat.

It was a lousy hike in, the occasional beautiful tufts of wildflowers or huge thistles offering the only color against a palette of brown and black rock and dirt. I met a few hikers coming out who volunteered that they finally gave up and never made it to the oasis. I began to wonder if it really existed, or if it was simply a euphemism for something else, like a little stream, barely noticeable to the average hiker. I thought about turning back myself, but then I crested a hill and saw it in the distance.

It had to be a mirage, for there in the middle of nothing but washed out desolation were monstrous palm trees, lush and wet and green. *Impossible!* Behind the oasis rose a steep wall of scree, and I watched as mountain goats scurried up the almost 90-degree slope. When I arrived at the oasis, the air temperature had dropped significantly, from 92°F to about 74°F. The stream not only fed the palm trees but provided water for birds, lizards, and goats and delicious cooling for my overheated body.

I sat in the shade near a clear pool of water and was as quiet and as still as I could be. Birds came to drink. Butterflies lighted on my knees. Lizards and snakes scurried by. I drank it all in through my pores before I began the hot, dusty hike back.

A few hours of reluctant driving later, I arrived in Palm Springs and grudgingly checked in at the conference resort, a beautiful place but so terribly fake. It was sickening, really, after having left the desert where the beauty is sublime and real. At the check-in desk, I'd spoken my first words in two days, and it felt like a death. Walking to my room—a whitewashed, tile-roofed bungalow set amid gardens—I felt like a feral cat, nervous, jumpy, and suspicious of everything. Scruffy, with wind-tossed, crazy-looking hair, I sidled past golfers, women going to or coming from spa appointments, children running across the grass in designer clothes. The sidewalks were lined with orange trees bearing fruit, but the trunks had been painted white. I wanted to *screeeeeaamm!*

My room, ironically enough, was called San Quentin. I literally locked myself in this cell for several hours before I could summon the will to step outside again and reconnect with the hectic pace of my real life. The vow of silence had cleared my head, allowed me to notice all the details around me and think with a clarity that was refreshing. Out in the desert, I began to appreciate the beauty of spareness, how much easier life would be if I could just get rid of all the junk clogging my head and my life. Here at the resort, with all its frippery and forced, wasteful greenery, I felt despondent. I hated it. *Remember this feeling,* I chided, *it's trying to tell you something.* But by the end of that day, having washed off the dust of the desert, brushed out my hair, donned a dress suit and high heels, applied makeup, eaten in a chandeliered ballroom, and listened to endless presentations, I was back in the grind and—sadly—it all felt completely normal.

How quickly we revert to a comfort level with tedium, I thought. Let it serve as a warning not to be seduced by the mundane. Two days later, when the conference was over, I returned to the desert to watch the wildflowers blooming. I was back again in silence, in nature, with ants crawling on my legs, storms threatening overhead, and all things completely unpredictable. But real. I'd found my center again. I was happy.

Chasing that feeling of happiness I felt in Joshua Tree led me to a commitment to spend more time exploring the wilds of North Carolina. On a local hike along a new ridgeline trail connecting Crowders Mountain and King's Mountain in North Carolina, the sun shone in a blue, cloudless sky, and the early spring trees were only just yawning awake. Without foliage to block the view, vistas spread out below the ridgeline on either side—one toward the Blue Ridge Mountains, the other toward Charlotte and beyond. I stood for a moment to appreciate the 360-degree view when a young woman walked by, striding with purpose, bopping to the rhythm of an iPod playing in her ear. She didn't even notice me.

More than a dozen turkey vultures soared on the thermals, so I sat on a rock to watch them and thought about the girl I'd just encountered—how she was squandering her silence, filling it up with noise. She was an energetic example of the difference between using solitude for introspection, or avoiding it by filling it with distractions. People ask me why purposeful solitude doesn't work when you've got music going. Here's my answer: We've got a finite amount of energy and it can only go in so many directions before it's completely diluted. If that girl is listening to music and trying to think at the same time, part of her brain is registering the music, the lyrics, the beat. That's taking precious gray matter away from the task at hand, which is to be thinking about her stuff, about life. Going deep is a process; it requires a lot of sustained attention and energy.

It requires solitude and silence.

Not everyone wants to think deeply about their lives, their choices or lack thereof, about the trajectories they're on, but eventually we will all have to. Better to do it now when we can do something about whatever it is we need to discover, than to have to do it when life is coming to its closing point and we don't have any hope for changing our course. "I wish I'd done . . ." at the end of life are the saddest words ever spoken; regret is the most desolate feeling in the spectrum of human emotions.

As I sat on the warm rock overlooking hundreds of miles of tree canopy barely beginning to turn green, I thought back to that moment on Tomales Point when I realized I had too much baggage, and what the promise to pack lighter has ultimately meant in my life. Through my expeditions in solitude, I've dropped the rough stones of regret, blame, grudges, unnecessary worry, and unrealistic expectations. Now, even the worst of my day-to-day life feels relatively unburdened compared to before. Not only had I been carrying too much with me on the path to a destination that didn't exist—a perceived happiness that was tied to another—I didn't even know I was lost.

I remember what I'd thought about during my walk in the fog, the concept of believing in what we can't see, the kind of faith you embrace when you're on an unfamiliar road without a map. It's easier to fret about being lost than it is to have faith in a future that will reveal itself only when you're ready to see it.

Solitude has given me exceptional gifts these past ten years. Far beyond the extraordinary moments with nature, the many hours alone showed me how to be completely present in the moment and gave me the time to find my center, the confidence to map my course. Solitude helped me find my compass and the mental space I needed for the next critical step, the most important one, the most difficult, and the *only* one that will help you navigate your way out of the dark woods when you find yourself there: introspection.

EXERCISES

WHY SOLITUDE?

Solitude is the first essential, a beginning. It sets the stage for what comes next. Solitude is meant to create a quiet place in daily life where you can begin to *notice*. Approach the idea of solitude not as deprivation but as revelation. Carving time in your life for regular solitude should become a habit, and an enjoyable one. Initially, ask for nothing from solitude except undistracted time to begin *noticing*.

As the word "solitude" implies, you need to be alone in order to reap its benefits. That means a temporary disconnection from all extraneous distractions, *especially* technology and, of course, other people. Whether your solitude will be one minute or one day, turn off and turn away from everything that has the potential to pull you out of seclusion.

Take stock of how much solitude you have in any given day. Driving to work? After the kids leave for school? Do you ride a bike for exercise? Golf on your own? Are you spending time watching television? Do you have a few hours before bedtime when you're by yourself? Add these up: You likely have a sum of time that equals solitude. Identify your opportunities for alone time, then begin to use them with more intention.

EXERCISES IN SOLITUDE

Slow Down

Take a moment each morning before starting your busy day to stand outside and just be still. Every single day, the sky will look different, the birds will sing in different patterns, the air will carry with it some scent from close by or far away. Feel the temperature. If there's a flower nearby, smell it. Look at the canopy of the sky around you and notice. Breathe in deeply and *notice*. Observe, too, how you are feeling. You don't have to do anything about it, just notice. You need to devote only a few minutes to this process, but if you do it three times a day—at the beginning, middle, and end of your routine— you will cultivate the habit of quieting your mind and separating it from distractions. You'll also become aware of your internal state, which is a clue you'll use later during introspection and commitment.

Study Details

Visit a museum or botanical garden, or take a walk on a greenway or a different route through your neighborhood. Spend as much time as you can indulging your senses in all the details around you. You don't need to think about anything except what you're seeing and hearing. Right now, you are simply cultivating the habit of carving out solitude so you can appreciate the moment, learning to be open and receptive for what will come later.

Make a Mindful Commute

For many of us, the daily commute constitutes the biggest chunk of our alone time. Sadly, this is not the ideal environment for maximizing solitude, because commuting tends to be frustrating, stressful, and distracting, but if it's all you've got, then by all means use it. At least once a week, disconnect Bluetooth, put the cell phone in the trunk, turn off the radio. While driving, notice the sounds of your car and the traffic whizzing by. Notice how you're gripping the wheel, feel where your body makes contact with the car seat. Is your breathing deep or shallow? When stopped at a light, feel the road shake, watch how fast everyone is going, try to imagine how many lives and stories are passing before you. Notice where your mind keeps going. But please, do keep your eyes on the road.

EXERCISES TOWARD INTROSPECTION

A healthy relationship with solitude lets you progress to the next essential, which is introspection.

Plan Ahead

Once in a while, expand the pockets of solitude in your daily living. Make a commitment that once or twice a year you'll give yourself some significant alone time. Every person should do this outside of their religious or spiritual practice so that the alone time is agenda free. It can be a trip, a day of "quiet time" or a vow of silence, or it can be a month traveling with nothing but a backpack.

Learn to Listen

At any point during the day or night, in any place, anywhere, you

162

can just stop and listen. Hear everything: rain, birds, night sounds, day sounds, dogs barking, children playing . . . You must cultivate an ear for listening in order to be ready for introspection. Learning to be still in your body and mind will allow you eventually to "hear" the voice that's deep inside you, that's trying to break through the noise and chaos to get your attention.

CHAPTER FOUR

INTROSPECTION

Introspection helped me recognize that fear had hijacked a big part of my life, but it also helped me figure out a way to take back control.

FRESH BLOOD SPURTED from the dog's neck, spraying chaotic arcs across the snow. One of the lead dogs in my sled team had turned on the other in a vicious, surprise attack, and now the whole team—six dogs in total—was tangled in a panicked mess. The dogs closest to me (and farthest away from the attacker) waited patiently for me to fix things, but the two middle dogs, in close enough proximity to the aggressor to fear her wrath, cowered on the snow, whining.

This is great, just great. I had no idea what I was doing. The other sled teams were well ahead and wouldn't come back until someone thought to glance over their shoulder and notice us missing. The injured dog could well be dead by then. I realized I didn't even know his name.

All of the dogs on my team were marginally domesticated. They respected their trainers, but were merely tolerant and sometimes disdainful of "guests." The guide had warned me about interacting with them during a high-stress situation. *Their stress or my stress,* I wondered as I searched my pockets for something that could double as a tourniquet. To apply it, I'd have to step off the sled; with nothing to serve as an anchor, the dogs could run away and I'd be stranded in the middle of the white, cold, northern Minnesota wilderness.

It occurred to me that since the team was tangled in their lines and one of the lead dogs was bleeding profusely, it wasn't likely that the team would be going anywhere. Gingerly, I stepped off the back of the sled, and, at hearing my first crunching footstep, the attacker growled. *Don't show fear,* I told myself, walking purposefully through the ankle-deep snow and over to the injured dog.

It was only because the attacker was harnessed that I didn't end up needing emergency first aid, too. As soon as I reached out to apply pressure to her teammate's neck, she flung her body at me, barking and snapping. When she came at me like that, all I could see was the glistening white of her blood-streaked fangs and the pink insides of her mouth. The harness and lines stopped her in mid-thrust.

"*Bad dog!*" I barked, but it was too late. When she'd lunged at me, I fell on my rear in the snow.

She had me right where she wanted, but my attempted interference incited a whole new attack on her teammate. She pounced on him, biting into his shoulder. Panting, the defeated dog lay there while the blood no longer spurted but seeped into the snow beneath him.

I had no choice but to watch him die.

THERE HAD BEEN so many dark premonitions hovering like ravens around this dogsledding trip, not least that I'd found out less than a month before that I would be losing my job. Plus, I hate cold weather, and 13 years of living in Buffalo, New York, earlier in my career had smothered me with enough snow to last the rest of my life. To top it all off, Minnesota was having a bout of bad storms, with flights being canceled every minute. I felt sure I would be stranded somewhere hellish, in the dead of the mid-western winter, alone, in the middle of some epic and historic power outage. But despite delays, tight transfers, missed shuttles, and lost paperwork, I made it to Duluth unscathed. Grateful that the roads were plowed and the day was clear, I could start letting go. Some of the dark omens ruffled their feathers and took wing.

Duluth to Ely was an easy drive, which gave me plenty of time to feel sorry for myself. Bitterness, I realized, was souring my taste for everything, but I couldn't help it. I was not losing my job because of poor performance but because of an impending merger. An ill-advised merger, in my opinion. I would join the jobless the year I turned 50. *Well,* I thought sarcastically, *that's one way to celebrate a milestone.*

I could feel resentment building into something formidable. Why hadn't I booked a winter trip on a beach somewhere, or a tropical island? What in the world had possessed me to pay hard-earned vacation money to hang out in the snow for a week?

With daylight to spare, I arrived at the lodge, where my "luxury" room awaited. After checking in, I trudged around in the snow to find my sanctuary and realized immediately that "luxury" meant a roof and that was it. Like many small vacation lodges that were formerly tourist meccas and are now holding on for dear life, the place was old, incoherent, and quirkily appointed. My "lodge suite" was really just a dingy motel room with a lovely deck and a spectacular view of a lake, yet there was nowhere to put my clothes. Theoretically, there was a functional kitchen, but inside the cabinets were cut-crystal pickle jars, no dinner plates. A television would have been an anachronism in a place like this. The lemon yellow, wall-mounted, rotary-dial telephone was straight from the eighties, and so was the phone book. I guessed I was lucky. Most of the units had no phones, though some had two-person hot tubs. I didn't need a two-person hot tub. I needed a way to call for an emergency evacuation to take me back to civilization.

The mattress, at least, was inviting, and I lay down to take a nap. Not long after, there was a knock at my door. It was Randi, the guide, advising that dinner plans had changed. It was hard to tell what Randi really looked like, bundled up as she was from stem to stern. She was short, that I could see, but was she heavyset or just well insulated with protective clothing? Her cheeks and the very tip of her nose were a bright and healthy pink. Her eyes were the color of a blue summer sky, and, although she was younger than I by at least five years, the blue was framed by the crinkles that come from a lifetime of squinting against the glare of sun and snow. Was she a little bit mannish? I couldn't tell under all that thermal gear. She seemed pleasant enough, but there was the slightest hint of forced friendliness. I was a customer, after all, and it was her job to make me happy (poor thing). In retrospect I realize it took me a rather long time to invite her in. When I did, she stomped her feet, three times each side, to dislodge the snow from her boots. There were two other people on this trip, she reported, and they had a cabin below me on the lake. Dinner

was supposed to be there, in the supposedly more posh environment, but they didn't have an oven (add that to the list of quirks),
so Randi asked if I could host the meals in my room.

"No problem," I answered, although I was secretly thinking,
What kind of operation is this? Just as quickly, I told myself to
stop being so reactive and to welcome the unexpected. *You're too
closed off. If there was ever a place to chill, this is it.*

Randi left and I was drifting off to sleep again when another
knock pulled me out of my attempted coma. It was Denise, the
chef. I watched as she whipped together an asparagus, ham, and
sun-dried tomato lasagna and slid it into the Flintstone-era oven
to bake. She also left me with salad, garlic bread, and a cheese-
cake drizzled with fresh raspberry sauce.

"You expect all this still to be here when the others arrive?" I
asked. She touched my arm gently, laughed, and left me all alone
to return to my nap, enveloped by the warmth and smells of dinner coalescing in the oven.

I got a head start on the wine before anyone else arrived, set
the table (yes, I had a dining room table but no bathroom towel
racks), straightened up the mess I had already made, and waited
for the next knock, which was Randi's.

"The others should be here any minute," she said, stomping
her way in. I asked for the lowdown on the other two guests,
but she couldn't give me much. A couple. Man and woman.
They arrived shortly after my 20 questions. I assumed they knew
the drill—they were coming into my room for dinner, but they
didn't say hello, or thank you, or even look at me, for that matter. After removing their snow-covered boots, they walked over
to the table and sat there, expressionless. I made a ruse of helping

Randi with the garlic bread and cast her a sideways glance with some eyebrow action. She shrugged. *Maybe they're uncomfortable,* I thought, *maybe they're feeling like they're imposing.* So I offered them wine.

"We don't drink wine," the Woman announced, annoyed, as if I should know.

"Beer, then?" I asked.

"Beer, yes," she answered and I served two. No thanks or gratitude was forthcoming, nor any eye contact. The Man looked like he was getting ready to endure a prostate exam.

While Randi was stirring and tossing and getting the lasagna ready, I tried to ascertain the details of my travel partners, but getting information out of them was like trying to drag a freight train with a spaghetti noodle. So I abandoned my efforts and focused my questions on Randi, who told us all about herself, her love for the dogs, for dogsledding, and for nature. She also explained why, as she'd neared 40, she'd chosen to forgo a decent income in favor of doing the thing she's most passionate about. As she spoke, Randi's face radiated a joy I rarely saw in people anymore. It was as if light emanated from her smile and eyes. I wanted to reach out and grab her hand, so that some of her aura would seep into me. But instead I thought about how I would soon be unemployed. *You need to figure out what will make you happy the way Randi is happy,* I told myself. *You need to do it soon.*

Dinner, despite the odd company, was really excellent. After everyone left, I took a pad of paper and pencil, thought about phase two of my life, and waited for ideas to come. It didn't take long for me to crash headlong into my pillow and sleep like the dead until the next knock on my door.

I had little trouble waking for Denise at 7 a.m. when she came to cook breakfast. I pulled myself out of the toasty bed and opened the door to an excruciating blast of frigid air that knocked me backward.

"Good God!" I hollered. *"Get in here!"* Denise laughed, stomped her feet, and shook her hat free of snow.

"Good morning!" She smiled, closing the door behind her. Denise had such a graceful way of intruding that I actually enjoyed being woken up by her.

Having given up my living area for the public good, I had only the tiny bathroom for privacy. I squeezed in there to change out of my pajamas and into clothes suitable for company. When I emerged, two extra pairs of boots stood neatly in a corner by the door, pooling melted snow water on the floor. The Man and the Woman had arrived, and Randi soon after. We ate breakfast quickly, but as we were preparing to leave for the day's adventure, Randi explained that the drive to the dog yard would take over an hour, over difficult terrain, and we'd be using our own vehicles.

"Do I need a four-wheel drive?" I asked.

"Not unless it snows," she answered.

"Uh-oh," I said. "Well, if I don't get there on time, send a search party."

I swear it took 15 minutes before the enigmatic couple offered to let me ride along with them. I had to choose: Risk being stranded in the snow or risk wishing I were.

OK, I thought, *these trips are about growing, getting closer to things. Abandon your rigid ways. Go with the buttoned-down, closed-off people. Maybe something wonderful will happen!*

An hour and a half of absolutely no conversation later, we arrived at the dog yard.

What an interesting place.

A hundred small, mixed-breed dogs lay in the snow, chained in front of wooden doghouses that sat at odd angles on short stilts above the snow. When the dogs saw us, they barely lifted an ear or opened an eye. It seemed a very laid-back place. Based on this apparent calmness, there was simply no way I could anticipate what was about to happen next.

Randi began our tutorial with a briefing on the mechanics of the sled. Knowing nothing about dogsledding, I paid close attention, but I was irritated that Randi was not showing us the reins. I ride horses. I wanted some reins to hold onto.

"Here is how you slow down," Randi explained. She showed us the piece of rubber tractor tire tread, about double the length and width of a shoe box, that dangles off the back of the sled and skitters over the snow unless you're standing on it.

"Step on this and it will make it harder for the dogs to pull. Now *this*," she said, showing us what looked like the business end of a leg-hold trap, "stand on this and your sled will come to a dead halt." *That's all well and good,* I thought, *but why can't I just pull on the reins? Where are the damn reins?*

"You will each have five or six dogs per team," she continued, "consisting of lead, point, and wheel. Harness your lead dogs first and give them the command 'Up tight.' They'll pull the harness mechanism forward so it makes it easier for you to harness your next four dogs. To go right, call out 'Gee' and to turn left, 'Haw.' "

"Haw, haw," I joked. "Randi, where are the reins?"

"No reins," she continued. "To start from a stop you say, 'All right.' Now," she said, her face changing from pleasant to stern, "it will be very difficult for you to get these dogs from their pens to the sled. I need you to listen carefully." Despite being completely distracted by the concept of not having reins to hold on to, I leaned in.

"These dogs are athletes. Very fit. They're not pets, and though they may look small, they can drag you like a dead squirrel. When I hand you a dog, grab it by the collar, lift it up, and walk it on its hind legs. Do not, and I mean *do not,* let its front paws touch the ground until you are ready to harness it."

I stood there and blinked into the snow. I just *knew* I would be the first one to screw up. I could feel it.

"Let me demonstrate how to harness your dogs," she said. Then all hell broke loose. As soon as Randi liberated the first dog from its chain, every dog on the lot sprang to life and began barking and circling in an unmitigated frenzy. I actually put my hands over my ears, but then realized I couldn't hear what Randi was saying.

"Hold the flanks of the dogs between your knees," she shouted, "while you slip on the harness. . . ." She showed us what we were supposed to do, harnessing her two lead dogs and then giving them the command, "Up tight!" The two dogs dutifully obeyed, walking forward until the lines became taut.

Randi smiled at me. "Ready?" she yelled. *Shit,* I thought, *I bet they love watching the numbskulls slip and slide through this part.*

My team that first day consisted of Bolt and Garmin (lead), Lance (point), and the two wheel dogs, whose names I never learned. They were terribly hard to lead, but once harnessed, they seemed to become rather aloof. Leading and harnessing the dogs was difficult work, and in the 20°F weather, I found myself shedding at least three layers of clothing and *still* sweating like it was summer in Florida. Eventually, we were ready: Randi's team in front; the Man behind Randi; the Woman behind him; and then me. Behind my team was our backup guide: slender, red-haired Natalie.

My team was still tethered to a tree when Randi's team bounded off into the woods. My dogs went crazy and Natalie shouted at me to get on the sled. If I thought things were loud before, they were just love whispers compared with this furious barking and yelping and yapping, which was as disconcerting as standing next to an air-raid siren in full-on mode.

"Janice," Natalie shouted, "*Get on your sled.*" I jumped on, put one foot on the brake and one foot on the sled bed, then turned to look at Natalie glaring at me, her freckles looking as big as pennies.

"*Get going!*" she shouted, and I could barely hear her.

"OK, OK," I answered, but suddenly could not remember the command to go forward. The team in front of me was gone, disappeared into the woods. The cacophony of the dogs was too much. It was like ten ambulances shrieking and a violent thunderstorm booming all at the same time. My prediction for screwing up had come true. Only I didn't think it was going to happen this soon.

"Janice!" Natalie shouted, "*GO!*"

"*All right!*" I yelled back, not meaning to but understanding that I had just given my team their permission. They took off as if they were going to take flight and I nearly flew off the back of the sled. "Holy crap!" I shouted, "This is *insane!*"

I had no idea where the first team had gone. Sled tracks veered off in every direction, so I just let my dogs run. They knew where they were going, and soon we were out of earshot of the dog yard. The crazed barking from the masses dissolved into the frozen distance. The three teams ahead of me were *way* ahead. My dogs were silent and working hard. Natalie was well behind me. I was completely alone, being pulled through a snowy wonderland by the muscle and sinew and good graces of five wonderful dogs. And suddenly, just like that, I realized why people pay hard-earned vacation money to do this crazy thing.

The wide, white trail suddenly narrowed into a path through dark and tangled woods. There were no sounds except for the light tinkling of the dog collars and the *shhhhh* of the sled runners on the snow. Once in a while, a tree cracked in the cold, or a crow made a funny clicking sound as I passed underneath it. Crisscrossing the trail were the tracks of deer and snowshoe hare and other, larger prints that looked rather menacing. I had only ten more minutes in this reverie before we caught up with the team in front. The Woman turned to me and said, with a beautiful and sincerely happy smile, "Isn't this *awesome*?"

"That's an understatement," I answered. The Woman turned away, smiling, and those would be the last words she spoke to me for the rest of the trip.

Until that moment, I'd had some trepidation about the whole dogsledding thing. While this was not the most dangerous trip I've taken, bad things *could* happen. Sleds could flip (with you on them). I could fall off the back of my sled, lose my team, and succumb to exposure before the rescue team found me. Frozen lakes could crack just wide enough to swallow me into their inky blue coffins. But as we sped along through the quiet of the dense forest, I decided that in comparison, this was probably one of the easier adventures I'd taken.

By the time we stopped for lunch on a frozen lake, I realized that even though other people were around me, for the most part this trip was going to be a solo thing. I would have a lot of time to think. There was so much distance between the teams, and the snow muffled everything but the sound of the sled. The path ahead opened up like a blank sheet of paper. It was time to write a new future.

Lunches were truncated affairs, the wind combining with the frigid temperatures to make relaxing impossible. We didn't sit around discussing politics or religion or the pros and cons of cosmetic dentistry. We ate coconut Thai soup, piping hot when poured but ice cold just minutes later, and cranberry cookies baked that very morning. Once done, we quickly organized our teams and got back on track.

Connecting the vast frozen lakes were trails appropriately nicknamed for the challenges they presented: Rock 'n' Roll, Surprise, Pinball. They were in complete contrast to the wide, easy sweep of the snow on the lakes. At the narrow, treed entrance to each trail, I'd have to abandon my thoughts and focus entirely on the task at hand. On all the trails, maneuvering the sled was difficult. I kept saying "gee" when I meant "haw" and more than once I almost tipped over. Rock 'n' Roll was bumpy. The sled jumped at every dip, half the time airborne, half the time banging down on the hard surface of the trail: *Bam, bam, bam,* for 20 solid minutes. I thought my teeth were going to rattle out of my head. Pinball was narrow, winding, and full of obstacles like rocks and trees. I tried as hard as I could not to hit any trees but stopped counting after I'd slammed into 20, every new collision adding fresh scars to the already beat-up sled. Long uphills required that we help our teams by riding the sleds like scooters—one foot on the sleigh bed and one foot pushing the sled along. It was hard work, but it did warm me up for a short period of time, important because my gear, though road-tested after 13 years of living in Buffalo, was not keeping me warm. In fact, I was so cold I felt like an ice sculpture.

Day one had been a physical and mental challenge. When we arrived back at the dog yard, our teams were exhausted, and so were we. The unharnessing went slowly and was much easier with the dogs not full of unbridled enthusiasm. Still, it was hard, sweaty, smelly work. Randi announced we'd be doing new trails tomorrow, with a whole new team of dogs.

On the long, silent drive back to Ely, dusk came slowly, like the spread of a water stain on paper. Neither the Man nor the Woman invited me to dine with them. Just as well. I had a lot of thinking to do and leftovers from our first dinner in the refrigerator in my room.

The wind howled as it curled around the building, and that was the only thing I heard until a Harley/snowmobile convention arrived. Although the lodge was barely occupied, the proprietors decided to house the majority of the bikers on either side of me. For most of the evening I lay on my bed, trying to read but being pulled out of the narrative by the boisterous laughing of my neighbors. Their happiness made me smile. Only snippets of conversation were audible, but I could tell they were happy to be with each other, to be free for a weekend from the droning monotony of their lives. I knew how they felt. Going home for me would be going home to the specter of a long, drawn-out, painful merger. Being stuck here in the frozen Midwest in an ugly room with paper-thin walls and a motorcycle gang on either side of me was entirely preferable to the fate that awaited me at home. *You need to figure out what you want,* I told myself, *because something is going to happen to you, one way or another.*

RANDI SMILED AS SHE handed me a pair of boots "guaranteed" to banish frostbite. They were military issue, white rubber covering multiple layers of sandwiched felt and a device to create a vapor lock. On my feet they looked like two miniature beluga whales. As I was admiring their ugliness, she asked, "Would you like a little more challenge today?"

"Sure," I answered. *How much harder could it get?* She said she was going to give me a dog that had a lot of talent but was also a little unpredictable.

Randi also gave me a different sled, noting with raised eyebrows the newly minted dents all over the one I drove yesterday. The new dog was a bit of an enigma. She didn't seem so much enthusiastic as determined. Something told me not to pet her. I harnessed her first and then went back for the rest of the team. She stared off down the trail while I attached the other dogs. Unlike previous lead dogs, she never looked at me, even when I was getting ready to give the command to go.

One by one the teams set out on the trail: Randi first, then the Woman, then the Man. I waited for Natalie to give me permission to go, but two of her dogs had chewed through their harnesses and she had to regroup. "Go on," she said. "Catch up with the others. You'll be fine. I'll come when I can."

With my new sled, a new team, and new boots to keep my feet toasty, I raced off into the woods. I already knew that the dogs would find the way; all I had to do was gracefully brake the sled as we turned one corner then another. With no one behind me or in front of me, the silence was delicious and I was all alone. In the treetops, I noticed something move and braked the sled. What was it? A great horned owl? A bald eagle? I waited for a while, to see if it would move again.

All of a sudden, the dog that Randi had offered up as a "challenge" attacked the other lead dog with such ferociousness that the hair on the back of my neck stood on end. The next thing I knew there was blood everywhere, and six dogs were suddenly trying to run in different directions. Within seconds, they were hopelessly tangled in the lines.

The female lead dog was in a frenzy, barking and snapping at the air. *Shit!* I thought and knew that I had caused this mayhem by stopping the sled. The stress of losing sight of the other teams had been too much for her.

If this had been a team of horses, I would have known exactly how to handle it, but I was in over my head. The female wouldn't allow me near her victim. He was losing a lot of blood, and quickly. Unable to help him, I watched what I thought was the last of his life seep into the snow. The other dogs heard it before I did— the sound of a team arriving behind us. *Natalie,* I thought, but it wasn't. It was one of the trainers. I saw him in the distance, jumped up, and waved maniacally for him to hurry. As he approached, he expertly disembarked and tethered his sled by tossing a slim rope around a small tree, all while the sled was still moving. "What happened?" he asked.

As I was telling the story, I noticed that the female was prostrate on the snow, and she had peed on it as well. The trainer growled some words at her. She responded by rolling on her back.

"What are we going to do?" I asked.

"*You,*" he answered, "are going to go on and enjoy your vacation. *I* am going to take Waldo back to the dog yard to get him fixed up. Natalie's on her way. She'll catch up with you soon."

He took my bandanna and wrapped it around Waldo's neck.

"He'll be all right," the trainer reassured me. "It looks worse than it is." Waldo got scooped up and deposited in the storage bin on the sled. The attacker, now pretending to be docile, was removed from my group and replaced with a dog from the trainer's team. One of my wheel dogs got moved to the front. All dogs seemed to be on their best behavior now that someone who knew what he was doing had arrived.

The trainer followed us for a while to make sure I hadn't been thoroughly traumatized by the attack. Knowing that Waldo was going to be OK was a relief, and soon I was enjoying the wide, tree-lined trail that wound gently through deep, dark woods. The trainer eventually turned around, leaving me alone again to catch up with the other teams. The silence was crystalline, like the icicles hanging from the trees. I was in the middle of Robert Frost's poem, "Stopping by Woods on a Snowy Evening": "the only other sound's the sweep of easy wind and downy flake."

Eventually the trail deposited us onto a frozen, snow-covered lake, and I saw the three teams up ahead, stopped. My dogs saw them too and doubled their efforts to catch up to their buddies.

"Everything OK?" Randi asked. "Where's Waldo?"

"We had a little accident," I began, watching everyone's jaws drop as I quickly moved to the most dramatic part.

"I am *so* sorry," Randi said. "I should never have given you that dog."

And I should never have stopped the team in the middle of nowhere, I thought. "It's OK," I said. "The trainer seems to think Waldo will be fine."

"What about you, are you OK?"

"I'm hungry," I answered. "Can we have lunch?"

We built a fire on the lake out of damp wood and moss, eventually resorting to a squirt or two of kerosene to make something happen. As bratwursts plumped and charred over the teepee of flames, I walked toward the center of the lake. Away from everyone and without a team to drive, I let the thoughts come.

I was soon to lose my job and the career I'd hoped would be my last. My family lived 3,000 miles away in a different country—Canada. I didn't have a second income, but thanks to a frugal nature I had a good cushion of emergency cash piled up at the bank. Some quick calculations and I realized I could live for three months on what I'd saved.

"Janice!" Randi called from a distance, "Lunch is ready!"

Walking back, I felt a sense of relief, but the matter wasn't settled. Something else wanted my attention, I could feel it. When we got back on our sleds, we had more than 20 miles to cover, mostly on long stretches of lake. I did my best to banish the nagging, jumbled thoughts and tried to focus only on the scene in front of me: dark fur against white snow, canopied by a gray and blue sky. But then came the question I knew I had to answer: *So you can afford to be unemployed for three months. That's great, but then what?* Here I was, in the perfect place to think about what was next, to write a new and uncharted destination on the vast, white tablet of snow. *What do I want? How do I want the rest of my life to go?* I had miles and miles of lakes and trails and two more days to really think this through. A little spark of excitement zapped me, like a tiny shock of static electricity. Buried somewhere underneath my confusion was the answer: I would use this time exploring the frozen wilderness to map a new future.

The next morning while harnessing the dogs—a process that was now becoming rote—I thought about the prospect of being able to afford to live for three months before finding another job. Was that what I really wanted? To find another job so soon? What would it be like not to work for a while, to be free of obligations and deadlines? To be able finally to organize my closets? Could I manage six months? As I clipped in the last wheel dog and patted him on the head, a smile erased the look of concentration on my face.

"What's so funny?" Randi asked as she passed, walking a sled dog on his hind legs.

"Actually, everything," I chuckled.

When my team shot out of the dog yard that morning, the sled seemed light enough to hover over the ground. All of the dogs were so enthusiastic and good-natured that I gained energy just watching their little backsides sway back and forth as they trotted happily along, tongues hanging out of the sides of their mouths.

We had another 25 miles of trails to cover. Some were wide and hard packed, others just barely wide enough for the sled and the dogs. On one open, downhill road I hung back from the rest of the team (but not so far back that the dogs lost sight of their buddies), then let them go as fast as they wanted. Randi had admonished us not to let the dogs run free on a downhill slope because of the danger of entanglement, but I couldn't help myself. One foot hovered over the brake, just in case, but the dogs were perfectly coordinated

and eager to catch up to the others, and we literally *flew* down the slope. You're not supposed to do this; you're supposed to always ride the brake on the downhill, but it was just too much fun to let them run—it was the closest I'd come to flying while still on the ground.

I felt something I hadn't felt in a long time—the spontaneity of being alive in the moment and taking it for what it is, the way we used to when we were children. Flying down those hills brought back memories of careening down the road in a homemade wagon with no brakes and no reliable steering mechanism and not caring what or who would stop me at the bottom of the hill. Back then it was enough just to enjoy the ride. The consequences, if there were any, were completely immaterial.

Nearing the bottom of the descent, I had to make a sharp "gee" and hadn't bothered to slow the dogs down first. So I went for it, and although I nearly flipped the sled, it felt like being a kid again. Adrenaline was making me giddy: I was *hooked*!

What goes down must come up, and the rest of the trails were all uphill runs. When gaining altitude, one of the things you must do to keep your team from becoming exhausted is to help them up the hills. If it's a particularly steep hill, you may have to get off and walk behind the sled, but mostly you help by standing on one runner and pushing off with one foot, similar to riding a scooter. This turned out to be as much of a workout as harnessing the dogs, and sometimes I would quit for a moment to rest. The dogs, I learned, were not having any of that. The minute I stopped helping, the lead dogs would turn and look at me. Talk about being shamed into doing your part. And by a different species, no less.

On the way back, as the clouds rolled in and the woods got darker, gusts shook the spiked branches of the leafless trees. It began to snow, all the flakes swirling softly in perfect diagonal lines. Suddenly, everything seemed to blend together and I gasped at the beauty. Out of nowhere, Basho's winter haiku came to mind: "In a world of one color, the sound of wind."

On our final day, the sun dominated the wind, bringing us crystal clear blue skies and 45°F temperatures. We met Randi and Natalie at the Filson Creek trailhead in the Boundary Waters Canoe Area Wilderness to take a day trip into one of its protected areas. Everything had been trucked in, but we still had to get all the gear organized and the dogs out of the truck. The harnessing and prep went smoothly and with a lot less noise. The first easy trail narrowed to hairpin turns where we had to portage the sleds by carrying them around extreme curves and over steep creek beds. The trails were difficult and I wondered why, on our last day, we were being subjected to such difficulty.

But then we arrived at Bogberry Lake, where the wide-open trail glittered and sparkled under the sun. There, on those vast, wide expanses of snow, I could relax and not worry about my sled, the lack of reins, or hitting some kind of obstacle that suddenly presented itself when I turned a corner. I could just be. And, because there were no distractions, winter's sublime beauty began, slowly, to capture my attention. I started to notice the details that subtly revealed themselves on that big, white canvas of snow. There was time now for introspection about my own life and about what was around me. Time to wonder what was awake and what was waiting under the four feet of ice beneath my sled. Buried under a blanket of snow and a thick cover of ice, the underwater world of a lake in winter must be very dark, and very, very quiet. It reminded me that I was about to enter a hibernation of my own—the death of one thing and the rebirth of another. Could I trust that spring would come?

Up ahead, I watched Randi drive her team. Occasionally when she'd turn her head, I could see her smiling. Here was a woman clearly in her element. *That's what I want, this is what I need to figure out. Once I'm free, what will be the thing that fulfills me? What will I be willing to sacrifice everything for?*

Randi stopped suddenly, and up ahead I saw what I thought was a moose trotting around in circles. Randi held up her hand, then turned to us and made a sign for quiet. We watched while the creature began trotting toward us. I squinted into the white-hot glare of the snow.

It wasn't a moose. It was a wolf, a big one, and it was heading straight toward us. We must have been upwind, because the wolf seemed not to notice us. The dogs seemed to be as captivated as we were and didn't make a sound. The wolf trotted closer and closer until I could make out the details of its body—the yellow tinge in its thick, gray coat, its dark eyes and large, adolescent paws.

Natalie got out of her sled—to get either her camera or a gun—and the wolf stopped. It stared at us for what seemed like a very long time before it turned and loped away, across the lake and into the woods. I'd never seen a wolf in the wild before and was so mesmerized I forgot to be afraid.

We were following the path of the wolf when all of a sudden the Woman's sled broke. I was never included on the full story about this. She still wasn't voluntarily speaking to me and no one was forthcoming with the details. It appeared that the frame went completely haywire, with the runners now sticking out into the snow at opposing angles. As the dogs tried to pull, the sled runners formed a V and piled up snow in front of it, creating a mound as big as a doghouse. Despite forcing the broken contraption to go a little farther, it was no use. We decided to stop and have lunch while Randi and the Man attempted repairs. We were in the exact spot where the wolf had disappeared into the trees. Its paw prints were *enormous*. The dogs seemed completely unimpressed by whatever wolf scent was left behind, and they enjoyed their usual lunchtime routine—flopping down into the snow and sleeping deeply while the humans dined on trail food.

Despite an abundance of duct tape, sled repairs were not progressing well. I asked if I could help, and when Randi told me to relax and enjoy myself, I told her I was going for a walk.

"A walk?" she asked. "Where?"

"Just around," I answered. "I want to take pictures of the wolf prints."

What I really wanted was to get back to the thoughts I'd been having before the wolf appeared on the scene. As I walked away, I posed the question again: *What do I want?* The word "freedom" kept popping into my head. *Freedom.* I'd been my own breadwinner for most of my life. What would it be like to take a year off? To be beholden to nothing and to no one. To travel. To write the book I'd always wanted to write? To rest. To be happy.

A year. *A whole year.* My heart quickened the way it does when you sense something exciting is about to happen. Could I actually do it? As I walked in circles in the snow, I crunched some numbers in my head. There was a lot I could easily do without. Certainly the "pampering" stuff could go. My car, though old, was in no immediate danger of expiring. No need to dine out when I was perfectly capable of cooking my own food. I didn't really need hardwood floors. In fact, the only things I couldn't do without were a roof over my head, reliable transportation, and my horse. When I added up the cost of those three nonnegotiables, they equaled freedom. And with that epiphany the last of the dark omens hovering over me took flight. I watched them fly away as I stood in the middle of the frozen lake, under the white winter sun, and knew that I had found my answer. The same light that had shone in Randi was now inside me. I could feel it. Freedom. There it was, up ahead, just waiting for me.

When it was time to head back to the truck, we drove our sleds at a walk, the Woman's sled still terminal. The slow trip back gave me time to imagine the new life I would create for myself. There were things I wanted to do, like go back to school, start writing a book. Everything, all of it, seemed entirely doable. The excitement of it all felt unbearable. I was ready to start my new life *now*.

At the end of our outing, we organized the gear and helped Randi lift the sleds onto the cab of a banged-up white work truck. With all the sleds piled up there, it looked like a rendition of the Beverly Hillbillies. The dogs were stuffed into tiny blue dog cages stacked on top of each other for the ride home. With one exception, none of the dogs on this trip had ever shown any aggression toward a human, but when I went to say good-bye to my team through the small breathing holes in their cages, they growled at me. Randi said it's because they're protective of their space.

As much as I hate the snow and the cold, I was sad that this trip was over. Winter has a sublime and brutal beauty that requires you to respond to it. There is something oddly compelling about the fact that the cold can find its way into you through a crack in your armor the size of a poppy seed. Winter is in charge, every moment you are in her grasp. I thought about how much careful attention I paid to dressing every morning, almost as if I were preparing myself for battle. I certainly was preparing myself for survival.

For a person who never wanted to see snow again, I came away feeling something different: Nature is complicated and profound, even when she is sleeping. Because I'd been traumatized by the long, Buffalo winters and the relentless gray drizzle of Vancouver, I'd purposefully avoided spending any time in snow or bad weather. But nature's lessons are not confined to one or two seasons. To have had the opportunity to rediscover this, through so many extraordinary moments as I was being pulled along by those wild and tenacious sled dogs, was an unanticipated but powerful reminder that we are never separate from any part of this world we live in. And when we try to cut ourselves off from it, as I had tried to leave behind cold and snow, some fragment of us goes into hibernation. Fortunately, that feeling of abandon we had as children—no matter how long dormant—can rise from its sleep fully awake and as ready to play as a puppy in the snow. It only needs an invitation. Or a sled, six happy dogs, and a wide-open trail.

Despite the fact that this trip was spare on many levels—the accommodations, the trail food, the size of the dogs, the conversation—I was leaving with riches I could never have found if I hadn't had time to send my thoughts looking for them. I might have come on this trip grudgingly, but I left it feeling more grateful than for anything before in my life.

The philosophy of the wisest man that ever existed, is mainly derived from the act of introspection. —William Godwin

KATIE SPENDS THE FIRST part of her day at the breakfast table, writing with a steady hand in her large, sturdy, leatherbound journal. The house is quiet; the chattering finches nesting in the hawthorn bushes outside the patio window punctuate the pauses between her thoughts. When her pen stops moving, Katie gazes off into the few uncluttered spaces in the room, looking for clearings where thoughts might appear. She'll often pause for a long time between sentences because she is trying to be clear. Katie is trying to sort things out. She's attempting to discover who she is.

Katie is 80 years old.

She is my mother.

"I wish I had started sooner," she tells me one morning over breakfast, setting aside the journal writing to focus on one of our rare visits.

"I'm proud of you, Daughter," she says, "You've done a good job figuring out what's important in your life." She hesitates. "I've decided I'm going to shed my labels—mother, wife, friend—so I can find out who's in here." She touches her forehead twice and then her chest—tap, tap, tap, tap—with an impossibly crooked finger. These words make me fidget because I know what my mom is in for. She's trying to tear off her outer persona to reveal the chewed up mess beneath. I've done it, and it's difficult work. Painful. Gut wrenching. I worry that it might send her into a spiral of despair. I'm happy that she's bravely embracing this looming specter of the unknown, but she's old and she might not have the time or the wherewithal to make adjustments once she figures out how she wants to change. And then what?

I look across the table at my mom: an old woman with a good, thick head of short, curly hair, black except for the faintest hint of gray, as if someone accidentally dusted it with flour. We see people we love the way we remember them, and so for a moment I have to look hard to see my mother's age. I can do it only by detaching from my childhood memories of her. This is difficult, but when I'm able to, I see 80 years of life etched all over her face and her hands and even her ears, and what I see is myself walking down that same path, 30 years from now. Like Katie, my war wounds will declare themselves as lines on my face.

Katie spent her life working in the garden, kneading dough for bread, sewing, cleaning, giving birth, subjugating her own desires in order to be successful at the two things she never really wanted to be: a wife and a mother. Her hands are as twisted and mangled as a car wreck, yet her handwriting is beautifully metered and strong, evidence perhaps of a certainty in the words she commits to paper.

"What would I have been if I hadn't married your father?" she asks the room. There is a long pause, so long that I turn my attention to the birds outside as they squawk and flit.

"What could I have been if I hadn't had you kids?"

I have often wondered the very same thing.

INTROSPECTION HAS BECOME suspect in our society. Often aligned with narcissism or self-involvement, it's either given short shrift or avoided altogether. But look no further than your own religious tenets and you'll see that almost all major religions either support introspection or require it. Think of the vision quest. Introspection is such a basic principle in that rite of passage that literally dozens of modern-day organizations have borrowed the idea. Now opportunities for modified vision quests abound throughout the United States, under the umbrellas of religious, spiritual, or leadership training. The value of a non-Native American vision quest lies not so much in learning one's true spirit name or finding one's trade in life as in figuring out your life's path. The reason it's called a "quest" is that you have to search for it. Whatever formal or informal quest you undertake, there is no question that solitude will be your companion, even if it's pseudo-solitude, like what I had in northern Minnesota.

In the Jewish faith, the Days of Awe begin on Rosh Hashanah, the Jewish New Year, and end with Yom Kippur, the Day of Atonement. Since Talmudic times (A.D. 70–500) this time was intended to be set aside for introspection and repentance, giving individuals an opportunity to evaluate their lives, actions, and inactions, to come to terms with mistakes and missed opportunities, to make amends with those they'd wronged, and to move closer to God. The ten Days of Awe encourage an extended inward view of an individual's personal landscape.

Lent serves much the same purpose, according to Frank Riley, a minister and navy chaplain who served in Iraq. "It is a time to ask yourself: What are the things that I am doing that I don't understand? I need to look inward." Lent is not just about giving up something that is hard for you to live without. If you love sweets and give them up for Lent, every time you crave a piece of candy, you are reminded to pray on and remember the Lord's sacrifice. It's a trigger, a reminder of that sacrifice, and an invitation to pray for what is needed in your own life, to ask the hard questions. "Introspection leads to deeper questions," Dr. Riley says. "What is it that I need to rid myself of? What is it that I need to know?" This ritual is intended to last 40 days, in deference to the time Jesus spent fasting in the desert.

In Islam, Ramadan is the annual month of fasting and prayer, not easy to endure if followed conscientiously. The ritual is designed to teach Muslims patience, modesty, and spirituality. From dawn to dusk, the distractions of food, drink, and sex are removed from the believer's daily life for 30 days, in order to create a kind of physical and physiological solitude that encourages deeper thinking.

Note that none of these religious practices are done in a day or when the person can easily fit them in to their overcommitted life. They include an element of suffering or deprivation, as with other rites of passage. From 10 to 40 days in duration, these religious rituals are drawn-out affairs, because it takes a while for thoughts to push their way out from under the layers we've stacked upon them. Once exposed, these jumbled thoughts take more than a little bit of time to unravel, to become, at the end of it all, epiphanies. This kind of introspection is not a selfish indulgence, and it's been recognized as a critical tool for spiritual growth ever since humans first wondered about the meaning of life.

Despite many years spent carving out time for intentional introspection, I have to be honest: I don't always like it. In fact, it's often so painful I'd rather lie on a bed of nails than scratch away for hours at my thoughts. What's to like? You think about things and then you know you have to do something about them. And the reason you haven't done something about them already is that they're hard problems. But what I like less is the idea of procrastination—that I'd have to start reflecting at a time in my life when I'd rather be content and not dogged by regret or "what-ifs."

Really, it's much easier to live with your head in the sand. But reality catches up with everyone eventually. So, what to do? Introspection won't happen if you're not "present in the moment." And if you've ever tried to be "present in the moment," you know how elusive that moment can be. Which moment is it, anyway? Is it the moment when you notice the sound of your breathing? The rain on the roof? The sounds of the traffic jam you're in? Have you ever attempted to focus, undistracted, on just one thing for a measly five minutes? It's no easy task to level your mind long enough for the marbles rolling around in there to come to a stop. Being in the moment, even for *just* a moment, is a feat reserved for the disciplined few who have practiced and mastered the art of scooping their mental marbles into a container and shutting the lid until it's time to bring them out again. With practice, anyone and everyone can do it, although it requires a sincere erasing of distractions—and it requires solitude—because you can't think clearly or hear your own voice if you're busy talking or listening to someone else.

Here's a piece of advice I'm going to share about maximizing the benefits of solitude for the purpose of introspection—it's the hardest to follow, but it's the most important. You must teach yourself how to be in the moment, and in order to cultivate the discipline for that, you have to come off the grid. Stash the cell phone, silence the iPod, stop checking and sending e-mail. Just *stop*. Whether it's for 15 minutes a day or the last hours before you go to bed, renounce the technology that is robbing you of precious time for introspection. Try to do this every day, eventually increasing the amount of time you can be silent and undistracted. Once a week, leave your cell phone at work and leave your home

computer alone. Turn off or unplug your landlines. Don't respond
to the doorbell. Don't even collect the mail. This may seem difficult
to do in daily life, but it gets easier once you recognize the benefits
of quiet time for introspection. Make, and don't break, a promise to yourself to begin. Beginning is the hardest part. Going forward, you'll add more and more quiet time away from the dreaded
ring tone, and that's time you can invest in thinking about what
you want your life to be. I find it much easier to break away from
technology when I'm traveling. If you are on a trip, give yourself
a grace period of exactly one day, 24 hours, from the time you
arrive at your destination until the time you renounce technology.
Tell the people who need to know that you've arrived safely. Tell
them again that you need them to respect your privacy, and let
them know that you won't be checking in, or checking e-mail, or
checking voice messages. Tell them you are, in fact, checking out.

I can't overstress the importance of this, and you must commit
to it. If the very idea of being disconnected makes you feel like a
junkie who's been told she has to give up heroin, then by all means
start small, but be *intentional*. Here's a compromise: make a promise to yourself that you will start and end each day in silence. You
wake up and you plan your day in silence. If you're on a trip, you
get to where you're going, and because you know you cannot be
interrupted by the dreaded ring tone, you can indulge all of your
senses on the landscape in front of you. You're able to immerse
yourself fully in whatever adventure you have planned for that
day. And you'll have plenty of time to think, too. Then, at the end,
when it's all over and you're showered and relaxed, you can call
whomever you want, tell them the kind of time you're having, say
good night to the kids, and then go back into your silence.

If you're journaling your trip, and you're serious about keeping up with it, wait until you're done writing before you reconnect with the outside world. Because once you start talking to your "obligated life," you will cease to be present, and your memories of what happened that day will begin to dissolve. Your experiences and memories of any given day are as fleeting as a cloud formation. Eventually, and *soon*, the shape will change, it will dissipate and morph into something else. If you want to remember exactly what the print of your extraordinary day looked like, you'd better draw it, write it, or photograph it before it's gone. Recording memories close to the moments when they formed is so important; it's a kind of introspection that has permanence. By journaling, you'll be able to revisit exactly how you felt in the moment when you felt it, and that in itself will be revealing to you not just now but years down the road. Journaling also allows you to walk back into those moments and relive them all over again. It's not just a tool for capturing time, it's a way to extend it.

All of this takes discipline. You either make this promise to yourself or you don't. There are no half measures on this one.

You aren't going to be able to be present in the moment *every* moment, all the time. Ordinary life *will* creep its sneaky, bothersome way back in and start shooting those mental marbles all over the place. This happens to everyone, even people who are devout in their commitment to meditation. Quieting the mind for introspection may take you so long to master, it might not happen until you're on your deathbed, but it'll never happen on its own unless you work at it. And working at it in solitude will give you a much better chance to get to the next place in your life, whatever destination that is for you.

This brings me back to the notion of suffering, which is something else we seem to try to avoid at all costs. For some time I've been fascinated by the Buddhist belief that "all suffering comes from desire." Desire, for me, had always been about expectations—expecting adults to be trustworthy; expecting the workplace to be fair and just and moral; expecting everything to go as planned; expecting always to succeed. Expectations, then, were causing me to suffer, in the form of disappointment, suspicion, cynicism, frustration. Introspection led me on a long path to the place where I could finally abandon expectations and instead embrace what is, expecting nothing between this moment and the next. Letting go brought a kind of freedom I hadn't expected, and it changed everything, from the way I run a company to the way I plan a trip. Not everything has to be planned to the nth degree. It's OK to have some ambiguity, an element of the unknown. Risks, now and then, are worth taking. What if I'd never agreed to give snow another chance? What if I'd never let the sled dogs fly down that hill? What if I'd settled for three months of freedom instead of a year? What unknowns are keeping you from pursuing the changes you'd like to make in your life, or the dreams you've failed to follow? What risks are you willing to take to move from where you are now to the place you want to be? Take some time in introspection to really, deeply think about it.

Religious rituals and rites of passage are helpful tools in deconstructing our psyches, but even without them, the need for introspection will come to us regularly in the form of loss, heartache, doubt. In every suffering we encounter, there is a hidden message. There is, in fact, salvation. A friend of mine, newly separated after 40 years of marriage, confessed that in his despair he spiraled into a dark place he didn't know. "I was a wreck, a complete mess," he told me. Angry, despondent, scared, and seeing no way out and no end to his misery, one night before bed he collapsed to his knees in tears, this tough man considered by everyone to be a pillar of strength. He'd been holding a book, given to him by another friend, which he'd tossed on the bed before burying his face in his hands. When he looked up, the book lay open to a page about suffering.

"Embrace it," the book suggested.

"What did you do?" I asked.

"I *did* embrace it. I let myself feel everything instead of trying to deny it. It was painful at first, but then it got interesting. It was a good way to learn how to find my way into a new life."

"Did it help you?" I asked.

"It brought me back. I had to go through the suffering to heal." The suffering, he now realizes, *forced* him to think about his life, to come to terms with the behaviors that had contributed to the end of his marriage, and, even more important, to think about the changes he wanted to make in his life going forward, so that he could eventually find happiness, or at the very least a semblance of contentment. He didn't really want to think about those things, but the anguish of wallowing in his pain was worse than trying to find a way out. Today, his heart is both happy and content. When he reflects on that time in his life, he wonders how he ever got through it, but he insists that the suffering, and the resulting introspection, were change agents for his life. Once he stopped railing against his pain and embraced it instead, his mind cleared enough to set some goals: to learn how to be OK alone; to have a richer relationship with his children; to spend more time savoring life instead of crashing through it. That was the work he gave himself; introspection coupled with action helped him start out on the path toward achieving those goals.

When I look back on the weeks and months following the unexpected and staggering news that I was losing my job and career at 50, I remember many emotions but was surprised at the absence of one: fear. Bitterness, anger, betrayal, confusion—they were constant companions for a while, but I never felt the crazy adrenaline of panic, the deep desperation I expected. And I knew why. Years of traveling alone had given me lots of time to think about how I was living my life. Going solo had crafted tools for me to use in daily life—a comfort with solitude, a recognition of the value of thinking deeply, and for an extended period of time, about anything and everything. Introspection helped me understand I'd been living life in too small a box.

When I first began traveling, 13 years before my eventual job loss, there were so many adventures I wanted to experience yet avoided because I was afraid of failing or of getting physically hurt. Look how long it took me to get into a canyon. Here were the questions I asked and the answers that had stopped me: Dangerous? Yes. Chance of major injury or death? Yes and yes. Thrilling and fulfilling? I knew it had to be. But even after trekking to southern Utah 13 times, full of intent and resolve, I couldn't bring myself to grab a rope and descend into the darkness of the narrow, cold unknown. Fear kept slapping me away from the edge. When I eventually fulfilled my dream, it took every ounce of fortitude I had—and inner resources I didn't even know were there—to get me through the terror and physical anguish of the adventure. It changed my life because it started an internal process of thinking about what it meant to be brave, how hard it is to be courageous at the moment when courage is needed, and how fear dogs us all during the length of our lives, often out of sight but always present. Introspection helped me recognize that fear had hijacked a big part of my life, but it also helped me figure out a way to take back control. And the way to accomplish that, I decided, was to force myself to do things that would scare the crap out of me.

After years of purposely testing my courage (and failing more times than succeeding), those experiences readied me for what I hadn't been prepared for at all: unemployment near the end of my working life. There was a lot to fear: homelessness, financial ruin, terminal unemployment. Hanging by a rope is the same thing as going out on a limb, which is what I decided to do by taking a year off. I never would have been able to do it if I hadn't trusted in the process of thinking things through, asking myself what I really wanted or needed. Or if I hadn't already tested myself over and over and over and learned that I could summon courage when I needed it. It was because of those experiences of wrestling with fear and holding my own that I knew, when the time came, I could be brave enough to take a big chance, one of the biggest a person can when they lose their job, their income, and their career: Take the time to do nothing and just see what happens.

EXERCISES

WHY INTROSPECTION?

Like solitude, this essential must be practiced alone. Devoting a portion of your life to deliberate introspection means that you will always have a "fix" on where you are—on how close to or far from your planned goal you may be—and an avenue for your inner voice to find its way to you. Use introspection in conjunction with the times of solitude you'll devote to yourself.

EXERCISES IN INTROSPECTION

Imagine the Life You Want

If you're not sure what you should be thinking about, start with the end rather than the beginning. Where and what do you hope to be a year from now, ten years from now? When your body can no longer reliably carry you from one thing to the next, what do you want to look back on and be proud of? We are going to assume here that the wish to be a good wife, husband, parent, partner, employee, and volunteer are givens. Think past those to what you really desire for yourself. If it's to reminisce and say you changed your little corner of the world, what will that look like? If it's to look back and say you finally got up the nerve to get up on the roof and clean the gutters for yourself, how will you get there?

Survey the Landscape

Identify what obstacles are obscuring the dream and blocking your progress. Somewhere in this overview, you'll stumble over some fears and fall straight into more than one "aha" moment. Recognize those fears, and ask where they came from. Here's a real-life example: I didn't understand where my issues with authority came from until I wrote the Baggage chapter for this book. What a revelation to finally understand why my buttons get pushed when people try to exert control over me. Through the writing—a very real form of introspection—I had an epiphany that helped me rip up yet another old script blocking my progress.

Prioritize

Once you have your list and your vision, distill it down to one or two of the things that are *most* important and take those thoughts with you on your walks, your drives, into your quiet times. Even when you think you've got the answer—as I did on the dogsledding trip, when I first thought about taking some time off work—keep thinking about it some more. Through solitude, you've learned how to listen and be receptive to your inner voice. You'll know when the *full and genuine* answer comes to you. It is such a feeling of revelation and release, there will be no denying its truth.

Persevere

This is not a process you can rush. It might take months or possibly years to discover what you're looking for. But it won't happen on its own. Take the first step and don't interfere with the energy of the process by imposing deadlines on it or yourself. Let it all unravel in its own time. Remember to be still in your mind and *notice*.

EXERCISES TOWARD COURAGE AND COMMITMENT

Once you've thought through where you want your life to go, it's time to pack your bags and head out on that journey. Whatever's been holding you back is about to be faced. Now you will have to learn how to summon courage. More than once. And often. (See chapter 2 and review the courage exercises before moving on to commitment.)

Discover

You surveyed the landscape and revealed the obstacles blocking your path; now identify which ones frighten you. Those are the obstacles you'll need courage to tackle. Start thinking about what it will take to get through, over, or around them.

Acknowledge

Recognize that your life won't become what you want it to be without some discomfort and difficulty. Acknowledge that you will likely have to sacrifice one thing for another. Begin to think about which few things in life—other than food, shelter, and love—are nonnegotiables for you. Keep the list spare. This will help you begin the process of unloading your excess baggage, so that when it comes time to summon courage, you're not weighed down by things that don't matter. It will be much, much easier to make a commitment to a new life if you're not dragging burdens behind you.

CHAPTER FIVE

COMMITMENT

No transformation comes from a place of comfort. Sometimes, everything has to dissolve before something new can be resurrected.

PERCHED HIGH ATOP a tiny trapeze platform overlooking the Hudson River, I quickly took stock of my surroundings. Here I was outside on the rooftop of an industrial building at Pier 40 in Chelsea, home of a venerable trapeze school; all around me the riggings of a trapeze apparatus and below me the net swayed like a giant, oversize hammock. I had only a moment to notice the Statue of Liberty to the right and Lower Manhattan to the left before adrenaline crashed through me like a flash flood, jamming my systems and narrowing my field of vision. Here was the iconic skyline of New York City, yet all I could see was the blinding white of the trapeze bar I gripped in my hands. The blood pounding in my ears silenced everything. Down below, reggae music blasted, people laughed and talked, horns honked, sirens blared—all the rich and jumbled sounds of the Big Apple. But it was oddly quiet as I leaned forward and listened intently for the command to jump: A single syllable, shouted with intensity: *"Hep!"*

There is only a first time once. When the coach shouted "Hep!" I leapt without hesitation, and the trapeze bar instantly hurtled me through the air. I swung way, way up—my feet pointing straight at the sun, feeling strangely weightless until the arc of my swing diminished to nothing, and my hands began to throb from their clenched hold on the bar. Every sinew in my arms burned, my failing grip the only factor keeping me from succumbing to the thing I dreaded most—free-falling into the net.

"Let go and fall," shouted the coach.

Letting go is one leap of faith. Falling is another. Having to surrender to both at the same time was more than I was capable of doing at that moment. I hung on, trembling, until my arms and hands couldn't bear it. Then, one blood-curdling scream later, I was bouncing on my back in the net.

I DIDN'T JUST WAKE UP one morning and decide to run off and join the circus for a day. I'd been thinking a lot about my last canyoneering adventure, which was at that time my ninth trip, and how I'd finally become comfortable with all of it; the heights, the ambiguity, the danger. Introspection after each adventure had revealed a really critical nugget of information: I do not have a fear of heights, as I'd believed for some time. My fear, it turned out, was and is a fear of the *edge*. This is an incredibly important distinction. Throughout my adult life, that perceived fear of heights blocked me from enjoying many things because I *thought* I'd be afraid. Realizing that my fear was more specific, more focused, and more explicable (what normal, sane person *wouldn't* be afraid of a precipice?) released me into a world of possibility I didn't think could exist for me. I'd lost many chances for adventure simply because I'd convinced myself I had a fear I really didn't have.

So, when canyoneering became relatively comfortable, I wondered if I had truly "conquered" my fear of the edge. How would I know, if the sandstone ledges and emerald green waterfalls no longer made my knees knock? I needed another test. Something different but equally fierce. A tandem jump out of an airplane, strapped to a copilot, wouldn't suffice—I wanted something that would make me take the leap on my own. After much head scratching, I came up with what I thought would be a respectable test—a session on a flying trapeze. It had both height and edge. I'd never done anything like it, didn't know a thing about it, and figured it had great potential to scare the living crap out of me.

I booked my trapeze lesson to coincide with the conclusion of a business meeting in New York City. The school was located on the rooftop of an industrial building on the Chelsea waterfront, only four miles from where I was staying. I gave myself plenty of time to get there, but I learned, as I sat in a cab in Manhattan gridlock, that there were going to be some hurdles to overcome before I actually got to take the plunge. Hurdle number one: getting there. It took one hour to go four miles. Honestly, a turtle with a limp could have made better time than my cab made. I was 30 minutes late and missed most of the ground instruction.

Hurdle number two: finding clothes that were tight enough not to shift and blow and expose parts of me while I was hanging upside down but not so tight as to reveal my deep, abiding love for double chocolate chip ice cream. I wore a pair of old leggings that did the trick but were, in places, threadbare. I hoped no one was going to be looking too closely.

By the time I arrived at trapeze school, the instructor was just finishing the orientation. A tiny, five-foot blonde, the instructor looked at me with one raised eyebrow and said, "Watch the others go first, then ask me if you have any questions." Since everyone was donning their trapeze harnesses, I did, too, mimicking their every move. The trapeze harness—a wide, thick, white belt worn at the waist—had metal rings at various locations around its circumference and was infinitely more comfortable than a climbing harness.

The instructor wrote our names on a dry-erase board next to the ladder leading up to the trapeze platform. True to her word, she scribbled my name at number six. I had five chances to watch everyone succeed or fail, and learn from whatever mayhem ensued.

Flier number five, a stocky, muscular man in his mid-30s, couldn't get his posture right. The net coach on the ground—a young man in his 20s—wouldn't let number five jump until he corrected it. "Lean out, lean out," the coach shouted. "Stop sticking your butt out behind you!" I squinted up at flier number five. *Please do something else wrong,* I thought. *This is the only instruction I'm going to get.*

With some extra help from the coach on the platform, flier number five got his act together and was finally given the command to jump. I noted a three- or four-second delay between the command to jump and flier number five's compliance. *No butt thrusting,* I instructed myself. *No hesitation when jumping. Try to be elegant for once.*

The instructions for dismounting the net were unclear, so I watched carefully while flyer number five crawled over to the edge of the net, grabbed two pieces of rope, and somersaulted off to land on a squishy mat ten feet below.

"OK, where's Janice?" called the blonde, erasing my name as she spoke. Watching me walk to the ladder, she was already shaking her head. "Take off those sunglasses and tie back that hair." Complying with her orders gave me a moment to take stock of my nerves. So far, so good. My hands shook a bit, my heart beat a little fast, but my head was clear and I was up for this thing. The first order of business was to hook myself into a rope attached to a guy wire that ran parallel to the ladder. Similar to the safety tether in canyoneering, the rope would keep me from falling all the way to the ground if I were to fall off the ladder. I looked up. Here was hurdle number three: climbing the ladder to the platform. The first 23 feet were OK. The last step onto the tiny, exposed platform was a doozy.

So there I was. I'd imagined what the moment would be like. I wanted to be able to slow things down, to take a moment, before I jumped, to remember the twin towers and the way they used to define the skyline in Lower Manhattan. I wanted to offer a silent tribute to those people who jumped out of the burning towers with no net to catch them. I wanted to hear and feel everything, the whole riot of experience. In a way, I guess, I wanted to both immerse myself and to detach.

But once I got up there, adrenaline took over, focusing me only on the task at hand, which was to organize all I'd observed from the ground into some semblance of order. I knew that a protruding butt would result in a lecture from the coach below, but when

"All right," the ground coach said, "crawl on over here. There are people waiting to fly."

On hands and knees I made my wobbly way to the edge of the net. It was ten feet to the ground but looked higher and scarier than the trapeze platform. "Grab the ropes here and here," explained the coach, showing me where to put my hands on the net, "then somersault off. I'll spot you." It was difficult, awkward, and it hurt my neck. Plus, it made me queasy.

"Work on your posture up there," the coach told me. "Try to look more like this." He struck the pose I should assume before the leap and I mimicked it, attempting to create a muscle memory that would follow me up the ladder to my next flight.

I got to swing three more times, and three more times I couldn't manage the knee hang. Luis, one of the instructors, took pity on me and offered a private lesson on the low bar. The low bar is just that—you only have to stand on tiptoes to grab it, but it's infinitely harder to work on than the flying trapeze. "I can't do it, Luis," I said, "I'm too old."

Luis just smiled and asked me to try again. He didn't speak very much English, but I'm sure he understood some of the epithets that were flying out of my mouth. I didn't like this part at all. It was too difficult, and my mind started to wander. There I was hanging upside down, grunting, flailing my legs, while a man held my waist with two hands. *Oh my God, is my underwear exposed? Is my ancient leotard ripped in all the wrong places?* I'm sure Luis had seen and heard everything, but at that moment the unintended exposure of my buttocks suddenly became more of a crisis for me than getting my legs over the damned evil bar.

Eventually, with much effort and noise, I got my legs up and over and hung upside down for a while as Luis rested his warm hand on the small of my back. "Come up," he said after a bit, requiring me to perform a single, herculean sit-up. This is where one would benefit from having really excellent abdominal muscles. I blame my difficulties on ten years of dedicated consumption of Girl Scout Thin Mints, which, apparently, had decided to take up permanent residence in my midsection. Nevertheless, Luis congratulated me and I followed him back up the ladder to try the leg hang in midair one more time.

While climbing the ladder for the fifth time, I felt a bolt of panic stab me in the heart. "What?" I said aloud, "*What?*" How could I have done this thing four times already and now suddenly be hemorrhaging from fear? It wasn't the fear of failing—I really didn't care if I managed the knee hang or not—it seemed as if that old *perceived* fear of heights had popped out of nowhere, like a leering jack-in-the-box. I shooed it away as best I could, but it kept skulking around in the shadows, mocking me. At the platform I took stock: my breathing was shallow and I couldn't look down. Not a good sign. Luis unclipped one set of safety lines and attached me to another. The platform suddenly became twice as small. I grabbed one of his arms to steady myself. He smiled as he adjusted my harness.

With both his arms around me, I noticed the details of his face: brown eyes, long black eyelashes, a day's worth of stubble, and a head full of dark, lush hair. I could feel the heat off his neck and smell his shampoo. It grounded me. I closed my eyes for a long time before I opened them again. He finished adjusting the harness and smiled but kept his hands on my hips. There was just the tiniest space between his face and mine. Deep in his eyes was a sadness, as if somewhere along the road Luis had lost something important and had never been able to find it again.

He looked pensive for a moment, then told me age was not a barrier to doing well on the trapeze. "Look at me," he whispered, "I am 40 already." He confessed his age like it was some terrible secret. I didn't want to tell him I'd passed that milestone some time ago. I thought of offering up some shallow chitchat but understood I was just distracting myself from the real flirtation— my last swing. *Stop procrastinating*, I thought, *just get on with it.*

Luis offered final instructions on the knee hang before I jumped, and this time I succeeded—one leg at a time—and it wasn't pretty, but I got both legs over and swung from my knees, upside down, seeing sky, wire, and platform upside down. Once I got my rhythm, I didn't want to stop. The ground coach commanded me to come up. When I was upright, he told me to perform a somersault dismount.

"No I won't!" I shouted.

"Yes, you will!" he yelled back and started barking commands that, surprisingly, I followed without hesitation. I flipped, head over heels, and landed perfectly, much to my delight and surprise. I *loved* the somersault and couldn't wait to get back up there to do it again, but sadly, that had been my last swing. I wished I'd been braver sooner.

The last part of the day was the "flying catch." It was by invitation only, and only for those fliers who could execute a perfect knee hang quickly and elegantly. I, it will not surprise you to learn, was not invited. Luis went from instructor to catcher. I watched with awe as some members of the group—a few of them first-time fliers—managed to let go in midair, trusting that Luis would catch them. Thirty minutes later, it was all over, and everyone was back on terra firma.

After thanking my coaches and giving Luis a hug of gratitude, I caught a cab to the airport. On the plane ride out of LaGuardia, I gazed down on Lower Manhattan, where the World Trade Center is now just a square stamp of concrete, and I remembered Philippe Petit's daring tightrope walk in 1974 between the towers. Celebrated in the documentary film *Man on Wire*, it was by all accounts an insane and really risky stunt, Petit himself not sure if he could do it and survive. But Petit had made himself a commitment long before that day in 1974 when he stepped out onto the wire and into the history books. His commitment was never to settle, never to become complacent with his achievements. He once said, "To me, it's really so simple, that life should be lived on the edge. You have to exercise rebellion. To refuse to taper yourself to the rules, to refuse your own success, to refuse to repeat yourself, to see every day, every year, every idea as a true challenge. Then you will live your life on the tightrope."

From the airplane window, I located the Statue of Liberty and used it as a landmark to find the pier I'd been flying above just hours before. What had I learned about myself in those moments, I wondered? Clearly, I was better with the "edge" thing. Although nervous, I was able to coexist with my fear, and there was never a moment when I thought I couldn't do it. Would I ever be able, I wondered, to find that balance between fear and resolve, a moment in which I could both immerse myself and detach? And really, would I ever want to? Hadn't all my best learning occurred when I was afraid to do the thing I had set out to do?

I felt grateful in so many ways for all of the freedoms I have, not the least of which is to put myself in danger, to test myself, to be crazy whenever I want to be. Grateful, too, for figuring out a way to open the doors that fear tried to close a long time ago. Sometimes, like the moment I was climbing the ladder to my last leap into thin air, I could hear those doors trying to bang shut, but they never quite made it. I realized that in spite of every test I'd faced up to, in the canyons, on horseback, in work and in life, there would always be something out there waiting to knock the foundation out from under me, and I'd never see it coming. I knew then, as the plane jetted away from New York, that if I wanted to live a life free of fear and regret, I'd have to keep testing myself over and over and over. I'd have to make a commitment to work at creating the life I wanted and the person I wanted to be, and I could only do that, I realized, by testing myself, *really* testing myself, every now and then.

The gem cannot be polished without friction, nor man perfected without trials. —Chinese proverb

WHEN I FIRST MET TERRY at a high school dance, all that really impressed me about him was his curly reddish hair and his freckles, which were more plentiful than mine. In the dark gymnasium, he smiled shyly, looking down at his sneakered feet as he asked for a dance. We talked a little bit, but certainly not about anything memorable. My best takeaway from that social was a raffle prize, Pink Floyd's album *The Dark Side of the Moon*, which to this day remains one of my favorite collections of music, and—thanks to the absence of headphones in our house—one of my parents' most despised.

But I remembered Terry, the boy with freckles who was shy like me. Our paths crossed a few more times, always when he was running training laps on the school track and I was riding my horse Rocky, illegally, on the school grounds. Terry hated running, so he'd cut away from the line of jogging boys to come over and say hello to me and chat a little before the coach yelled at him to come back, and at me to get my horse off the grass. The last time I saw Terry alive, he asked if he could take Rocky for a spin.

"Can you ride bareback?" I asked.

"I guess we'll find out," he answered. Grunting, I gave Terry a leg up, almost tossing him all the way over to the other side. "Ouch," he said, while settling into place on the horse's back; Rocky had a spine like a razor blade.

"You'll need this," I said, offering Terry the whip.

"Let me try without it," he answered, kicking and kicking at Rocky's sides to no avail. The horse just looked at me with eyes that left no doubt in my mind he was completely unimpressed by his rider's efforts.

"Seriously," I said, "this will make things a whole lot easier." Terry didn't want to hit the horse, so I did—one whack on Rocky's behind and he burst into a trot, Terry teetering off one side then the other as he tried to maintain balance by gripping fiercely with both legs.

"Uh-oh," I said aloud as Rocky mistook the pressure of Terry's grip for the request to gallop and took off. Terry managed to find a rhythm and was doing a pretty good job of staying on, but his arms were flapping so wildly he couldn't steer.

"Uh-oh," I muttered again as Rocky galloped straight toward an unmowed patch of field where the grass was chest high, green, and irresistible. Terry—not knowing what was about to happen—let out a hoot, waving one arm in the air just as Rocky slammed on the brakes and plunged his open mouth into the equine smorgasbord in front of him. I cringed as Terry somersaulted through the air. When he landed, he did so on both feet, looking incredulous at first and then nodding his approval. Smiling, covered in grass seed, he emerged from the tall weeds pulling Rocky along behind him.

"That was fun," he said, handing me the reins, "but I don't think I'll do it again."

I yanked the giant tufts of half-chewed grass out of Rocky's mouth, jumped up on his back, and gathered the reins. "'Bye, Terry," I said, as I cantered off. "See you next time."

But there wouldn't be a next time. Terry would soon face the biggest test of his life, and in doing so, become one of the most beloved and revered heroes in Canadian history.

Terry Fox was born in 1958 in Winnipeg, Manitoba, and raised in Port Coquitlam, British Columbia, a small community near Vancouver. Studious, serious, and shy, he was a good kid, smallish in stature—only five feet in junior high school—but he worked extra hard to excel at sports, even though he wasn't naturally gifted. Terry was crazy for basketball, but his coach, noting that Terry's persistence wasn't productive, suggested he try cross-country running instead, something Terry agreed to reluctantly and only to satisfy the coach, whom he'd come to respect. But he didn't excel at running either, and he found the workouts so exhausting he'd sometimes be afraid to start them.

Terry was determined to do whatever it took to make his way back onto the basketball court as a player, and his endless practicing and dogged determination paid off: By the time he reached 12th grade, he was a valued basketball player and shared the Athlete of the Year Award with his best friend, Doug Alward.

After graduating from high school, Terry enrolled at Simon Fraser University and tried out for the junior varsity team, which at that time was the best in the province, a fact that was more than a little intimidating to Terry. The two-week training camp was a kind of endurance test, a way for the coach, Alex Devlin, to weed out the weak and noncommitted. Devlin watched Terry closely, and although Devlin noted that others were more gifted than Terry, no one showed more desire or tenacity. Terry's hard work paid off again: he made the team.

Less than a year after graduating from high school, while enrolled at SFU, Terry learned that a persistent pain in his knee was caused by osteosarcoma, and on March 9, 1977, his right leg was amputated six inches above the knee. The night before surgery, Terry read a magazine article about Dick Traum, the first amputee to complete the New York City Marathon. For 16 months following that surgery, Terry endured the ordeal of chemotherapy, his time in a cancer control program in British Columbia both heartrending and transformational. Watching so many of his fellow patients suffer and die, Terry knew that if he survived, he had do something with his life that would or could make a difference. After completing treatments, he left the facility with new purpose. He'd credited his survival to recent medical advances, treatments that hadn't been available to patients who'd died only a year before. Terry's time in the hospital, in the special solitude that comes from facing death, led him to an epiphany he would never abandon: he would commit the rest of his life to raising awareness for cancer research and to inspiring other cancer patients to find the inner courage to fight the disease with determination and tenacity.

Remembering the story he'd read the night before his surgery, about the amputee who had completed the New York City Marathon, Terry threw himself into a 14-month training program with a plan of competing in a marathon himself. Or at least that's what he told his mother. Secretly, he was planning something much grander. His confidential plan, which he initially divulged only to his friend Doug, was to run across the length of Canada, on one leg and his prosthesis, to raise awareness for cancer research.

On April 12, 1980, Terry dipped his artificial limb into the cold waters of the Atlantic Ocean in St. John's, Newfoundland, and officially began his Marathon of Hope. Earlier, in October 1979, Terry had written to the Canadian Cancer Society, asking them to support his run. "I'm not a dreamer, and I'm not saying this will initiate any kind of definitive answer or cure to cancer," he explained, "but I believe in miracles. I have to."

Every Canadian alive during Terry's Marathon of Hope remembers his unusual and poignant gait, a kind of hop-step. He'd hop on his good leg, then step down on his prosthesis. The springs in the artificial leg needed time to reset after each step, so it was a measured, deliberate pace. The going was at times agonizing; blisters on his feet, bruises on his stump, intense pain all over. But Terry was no stranger to pushing his body past all reasonable limits. His earlier commitment to overcome natural mediocrity and become a star on the basketball court had prepared him for this moment and all the moments that ensued. Each morning Terry ran through 20 minutes of suffering before crossing a threshold of pain and leaving it on the road behind him.

Every day Terry ran roughly the equivalent of a marathon. He was committed to pushing through the shin splints, the inflammation, the cysts and blisters. He refused to take a day off, even on his 22nd birthday.

The Marathon of Hope was gaining momentum, but occasionally a community would fail to recognize history in the making. Terry's feelings were hurt, noting in his journal that he "tries so hard," yet no one came out to greet him. But these disappointments were erased by the tidal wave of affirming recognitions; for example, in Ontario, after a Sault Ste. Marie radio station put out the call that a spring had snapped in Terry's artificial leg, a welder grabbed his equipment and sped off to find him. Ninety minutes later, the spring was repaired and Terry was back on the road again. There was no question that at this point, the Marathon of Hope was inspiring millions of Canadians and others who were watching his audacious commitment in action.

Of course, I was one of them. The only reason I knew that Terry Fox was the Terry who'd asked me shyly for a dance, who'd been thrown unceremoniously into the weeds by my devious horse Rocky, was because of Terry's reddish hair and freckles, which set him apart from all the other people I knew at that point in my life. What I also can't forget is watching the television broadcasts of Terry making his painstaking, hop-stepping way across Canada, through wind and snow and hail and bad drivers, and recognizing the profound loneliness he must have felt. Images of him covering ground, foot by deliberate foot, with a police car behind him and thousands of miles of road ahead, underscored the solitude of his incredible journey and magnified the humanity of his commitment. It was impossible to remain unmoved by the sight of it.

By late August, four and a half months into his marathon, Terry was already exhausted even before starting each day's run. On September 1, an intense coughing fit forced him to stop just outside Thunder Bay, Ontario. Crowds lined the street, and despite pain in his chest, Terry decided to keep running as onlookers lined up on both sides, shouting encouragement. A few miles later, out of sight of the fans, Terry stopped and asked Doug to take him to a hospital.

The cancer had spread to his lungs. In an emotional press conference, Terry announced he would end his run after 143 days and 3,339 miles. Immediately, offers from others to complete the run flooded in, but Terry refused them all. He was completely and totally committed to finishing the Marathon of Hope on his own two mismatched, heroic legs.

On June 28, 1981, after chemotherapy and interferon treatments, Terry died at Royal Columbian Hospital in New Westminster, British Columbia, just shy of his 23rd birthday. Less than a month later, the province named an 8,658-foot peak in the Rocky Mountains Mount Terry Fox—a lasting symbol of his courage. Two weeks after that, a 52-mile section of the Trans-Canada Highway in Ontario between Thunder Bay, where Terry was forced to stop his run, and Nipigon was renamed the Terry Fox Courage Highway. On the same day, the Canadian government created a five-million-dollar endowment fund called the Terry Fox Humanitarian Program to provide scholarships to students who exhibited the highest ideals and qualities of citizenship and humanitarian service.

A month later, Terry was posthumously inducted into the Canadian Sports Hall of Fame. Two weeks after that, the first Terry Fox run was held at more than 760 sites in Canada and around the world. My father ran in this race, in shoes so old they were not fit even for walking.

There are, of course, many other examples of transformational commitment. Mother Teresa is one of them. Her commitment to serving and loving the marginalized people of the world makes her—according to Gallup polls—one of the most popular inspirational figures year after year. After her father died when she was eight years old, Agnes Gonxha Bojaxhiu (later known as Mother Teresa) spent time alone thinking about where life's path would lead her. She was transfixed by stories about missionaries and their service, and by the time she turned 12, had spent enough introspective time to decide that she wanted to commit herself to a religious life of service. Her pledge to serve the destitute required tremendous commitment and sacrifice: When she left home at 18 to join the Sisters of Loreto and begin missionary work, it was the last time she ever saw her sister or her mother. Later, when she felt compelled to leave the convent to tend to the needs of people living on the street, she found the work difficult and exhausting, and at times had to resort to begging for food and shelter herself. Later she had an opportunity to return to the relative luxury of the convent but refused. "Today I learned a good lesson. The poverty of the poor must be so hard for them. While looking for a home I walked and walked till my arms and legs ached. I thought how they must ache in body and soul, looking for a home, food and health. Then the comfort of Loreto [the convent] came to tempt me. 'You have only to say the word and all that will be yours again.' ... Of free choice, my God, and out of love for you, I desire to remain and do whatever be your Holy will in my regard. I did not let a single tear come."

It is hard to imagine a faith so strong it could persuade Mother Teresa to live in wretched conditions for most of her life, surrounded daily by reminders of the savage inequalities in the world. What's even more extraordinary is that Mother Teresa spent many years questioning her faith and the existence of God as she believed him to be. She wrote in a letter to a trusted adviser: "Where is my Faith—even deep down ... there is nothing, but emptiness & darkness. . . ." In a later letter, she lamented, "Repulsed, empty, no faith, no love, no zeal. . . . What do I labor for?"

Yet she continued her unreserved commitment to the segment of society she described as "the hungry, the naked, the homeless, the crippled, the blind, the lepers, all those people who feel unwanted, unloved, uncared for throughout society, people that have become a burden to the society and are shunned by everyone." Pushing forward in the face of doubt, finding inner resolve to continue despite her own suffering—her commitment is more than just inspirational, it's heroic.

Nelson Mandela is another example of how solitude, introspection, courage, and commitment—when they merge at the right time and with the right individual—become transformational. Mandela's lineage was royal, yet the South Africa where he was born refused to grant him the same rights as people who were less pedigreed but happened to have been born white. He had plenty of time to think about this disparity while growing up. His deep involvement in politics and the fight to eliminate apartheid eventually landed him in jail for 27 years. His classification in prison was D, the lowest, and he and the other low-ranking prisoners performed hard labor in the quarries every day. His cell was spare and depressing.

Meanwhile, Mandela was offered his freedom on more than one occasion, if he would agree to certain conditions that were contrary to his position on segregation and human rights. He flatly refused, despite the fact he could have lied, just to end the solitude. He was allowed to write and receive one letter every six months and could have only one visitor a year. His loneliness must have been staggering.

In prison, Mandela's commitment to pulling his country out of the ashes of its own violence grew deeper, as outside the prison walls South Africa unraveled in bloodshed, violence, and division among its people. When Mandela was finally released, in 1990, he went right back to work facilitating the end of apartheid. Isn't it astonishing that this man who had been jailed for treason against his country ultimately became its first black president, was awarded the Nobel Peace Prize, and has become a symbol of the hope for world peace? This is the same person who was denied entry into the United States until July 2008 because of his affiliation with the ANC—the anti-apartheid group he'd been part of. The ANC was officially designated a terrorist group by the country's ruling white minority, and other countries, including the United States, followed suit. When he eventually visited the United Nations headquarters in Manhattan, he required a special waiver from the U.S. secretary of state.

His commitment to creating a world of equality, dignity, and peace has been revolutionary.

But Mother Teresa and Nelson Mandela are really epic examples of commitment, beyond the reach of the common woman and man. It's the same with solitude and introspection. Few of us could or would spend months or years in nature and introspection, as John Muir, Everett Ruess, and the Japanese poet Basho did. We love the Winston Churchill type of story of courage, but I suspect most of us feel we can't rise to that level either.

But Terry's story is *our* story, and I chose to tell it because it perfectly illustrates how solitude, introspection, courage, and commitment—when they converge—can become something so powerful they transform not only the individual but others as well. One might argue that Terry's case is special, because he knew he had a limited time to make a difference. But don't we all? None of us know which day will be our last, which doctor visit will deliver the worst news of our lives, which accident will snatch us forever from our carefully constructed lives. I wanted to tell Terry's story because he represents the power that lies dormant within all of us. Terry was not a saint, he was neither gifted nor brilliant. He was just a guy—a *nice* guy—who worked hard and tried to do the right thing. But when life pushed at him, he pushed back, and in doing so inspired a nation. His commitment to living a life of meaning, to never giving up on the thing he knew was his purpose, reshaped attitudes, lives, and even policies. Terry Fox, the freckled, pleasant boy who reluctantly asked me to dance in the dark gymnasium, would become a symbol of hope for millions and an incentive for a government to focus more of its resources on finding the cure for a disease that continues to ravage the human race.

Terry was an average guy who hated running. Ironically, running is how he stamped his indelible presence onto the pages of the history books. And he did it through commitment, which came out of solitude, introspection, and learning how to beckon courage every day. His solitude was internal: You face death and heartache alone, even when you are surrounded by people. His long ordeal of chemo gave him time to be introspective. His challenge to himself, which would require enormous courage, was to make a definitive difference. He committed to never quitting.

WHY IS COMMITMENT IMPORTANT? Trials will come to you your whole life. Pain and suffering, as difficult as they may be, are essential for growth. You can rail against misfortune or you can say, "What can I learn from my pain? How can I grow stronger?"

Why wait for the test to find you? Start testing yourself on your own terms. Grow your capacity for resilience. Challenging yourself, building your courage muscle, and taking time to really deconstruct your experiences through introspection will help you become more capable of handling the next travail. Every time you throw yourself into the pit and emerge on the other side a little bloodied but still OK, you will be wiser. And braver.

When you make a commitment to spending time thinking deeply about your life and the obstacles you need to overcome, you'll see how the challenges change as you grow. What scares you at 20 won't be what scares you at 40 or 50. Create your own trial by fire, even in the small details of daily life, to forge and ready yourself for what is surely waiting around one of life's corners. It's not enough to do it once and believe you're done.

It's like faith or love. You wouldn't pray once and consider that sufficient. You wouldn't tell your children you love them and never say it again. The commitment you make to building the life you want will be the one that resonates for you. If your commitment is to better serve your fellow human beings, look past volunteering in your community and go, once in a while, to an impoverished region where you won't have the luxury of your own bed at night. Help out somewhere after a natural disaster, where no infrastructure remains and you have to live in the same conditions as the victims. You don't have to do it all the time, but doing it now and then will provide a context for being ever more grateful for the richness of your life.

If your commitment is to rid your life of toxic people, start now. Retreat from those bad relationships and spend some time in introspection to understand why you tolerate those relationships in the first place. In the context of this book, commitment is about two things: 1) committing to a promise that you won't settle for a life less than what you know you are capable of, and 2) recognizing that the life you want will come only after you give yourself alone time to really think things through, to figure out what your next challenge needs to be in order to make a difference somewhere, for someone, even if it's only for you.

Halfway through the writing of this book, it occurred to me that I hadn't tested myself in a while. Immediately, that little voice in my head, the one that tries to talk me out of things, said, "Come on, haven't you already done enough? Haven't you proved yourself to yourself?" "Yes," I answered but heard complacency echo in my answer. For once I tried to cut myself a little slack, even though I knew what was really going on: I didn't want to have to wrestle with fear again. The battles had become exhausting. But if I'd learned anything, I'd learned that when those internal conversations begin, it's time to spring into action, because somehow, some way, fear is starting to find a foothold again.

I had a trip coming up—two weeks in northwestern Washington State and southwestern British Columbia. I knew right away what I needed to do, something I'd been afraid to do when I lived in Vancouver all those years ago—a tandem paraglide off Grouse Mountain. The very thought of it made me sick to my stomach, before I even boarded an airplane to fly west. Once in Canada, during the four days leading up to my paragliding flight, I felt worry pawing at me like an anxious dog. On the morning of the big day, I looked out over Vancouver Harbour and saw that the top of Grouse Mountain was socked in with fog. Because conditions had to be perfect in order for paraglide flights to proceed, there was a good chance all flights would be canceled. I'd talked a friend into going with me and said to him, "We may not get to fly today," trying my best not to smirk. "Let's go for a walk in Stanley Park instead," I said.

There is nowhere in Stanley Park that you can't look across the water and see Grouse Mountain. As each hour passed, the peak became more discernible through the fog, until it pronounced itself proudly and fully against the skyline. *Shit*, I thought.

Getting up there wasn't easy, nor was it cheap. My friend and I rode the gondola up the steep grade of 45 degrees. Packed like a sardine into the crowded, small steel bubble that groaned and swayed disconcertingly every time it crossed a transfer tower, I was already having difficulties that seemed all too familiar. After the gondola ride came the chairlift to the top of the mountain. My friend was a skier, but I'd never been on a chairlift in my life. "How are you doing?" he asked, halfway through the ride, noting, I'm sure, that my face was drained of all color. As we were nearing the top, I watched as a paraglider set sail by running straight off the edge of the mountain and nearly entangling the chute in the lift.

Once I'd handed over my $275 ticket and stepped into a flight harness, preparations didn't take long and instructions were minimal. I watched as the pilot unraveled the sail—no solid frame, just half a parachute and tangles of lines. The pilot faced me forward and then snapped my harness onto his. Even though I knew he was there, I couldn't feel him. It was going to seem as if I were doing this thing on my own. "Walk four steps, and when I tell you to run, run hard," he told me. "I'll be right behind you."

Facing the edge, where I'd have to run into thin air, I heard the parasail rustle behind us, like a raven's wings opening to take flight. We began to walk. One, two, three steps, and I felt the tug of the sail pull me back. "Keep going," the pilot urged, "and *run!*" I ran harder than I ever have in my life and watched my feet as they whirled off the side of the mountain. I never had a sense of falling, because the sail pulled us skyward, up and over the chairlift, high above the trees, and into a space of air that revealed a dazzling panorama—Vancouver, Burrard Inlet, the Lions Gate Bridge, cities, towns, and the glittering Pacific Ocean. The day was now so clear I could see all the way to Mount Baker in Washington State. Below us, Capilano Lake shone with the deepest blue I'd ever seen, and poking up out of the mountain range behind us were the regal stone heads of the Twin Lions.

Whatever initial fear I had was long gone. I could see Burnaby Mountain, where I'd spent years of my young life on Rocky's back, exploring the woods and ponds and paths in my own little corner of the province. I knew then, as I saw the world below me in a new way, that this was why I had to make a commitment never to let fear win. Those moments of discomfort on the gondola, on the chairlift, worrying about whether I would be able to run off the side of the cliff—such a minor price to pay for this extraordinary moment of defying gravity, of seeing planet Earth below me the way a bird would see it, feeling the cold wind on my face, the scary exhilaration of being suddenly snatched and flung up by a thermal. My heart felt open. The commitment I'd made a long time ago—to stop letting fear make my decisions—had brought me here, to this indelible moment, to the very place fear had convinced me was off-limits for good.

"TODAY I ATTENDED THE FUNERAL of my former self," Jasmine told a group of 56 people she'd known for only two days, "and that funeral was for the person I used to be. I buried that person who was negative, who was unkind, who was unhappy. I have made a promise to myself that she is dead forever."

Jasmine, a 33-year-old African-American single mom, a former Olympic weight lifter-in-training turned marketing consultant, is the picture of serenity. Her kind brown eyes and pretty smile highlight a face that exudes depth and intelligence. Her physical strength is undeniable—in her heyday she could lift 85 kilograms (187 pounds) in what lifters call the clean and jerk and 80 kilograms (176 pounds) in the snatch. Her upper body is an attractive combination of a weight lifter's bulk and a woman's curves. Despite being divorced and a working mom,

Jasmine seems to have it all together. And no one with any sense of self-preservation would ever question Jasmine's obvious physical power.

Yet Jasmine is afraid of heights, and recently she had to navigate a high-ropes course as part of a leadership development retreat. I was stationed as photographer on the third platform of the "sieve," a medieval-looking wooden tower that, at each of its three upper levels, led to all kinds of cabled tortures. Jasmine's breathing announced her arrival long before I actually saw her. Those deep, deliberate in and out breaths, like blowing into a balloon, signaled distress. As if a tuning fork had been struck, my breathing began to mimic hers. When she appeared on the platform below, the fear in Jasmine's eyes triggered in me every horrible memory of my own battle with heights and the edge. Watching as she willed herself to take one step then another— her eyes staring straight ahead but seeing nothing—I felt sick and suddenly woozy, even though I was clipped into the cables and perfectly safe in my position on the platform. When she hoisted herself up to where I stood crammed in the corner to get out of her way, I wanted to grab both her hands, to hug her, to tell her she would be just fine. But I knew she had to work this thing out on her own.

I'm not sure that Jasmine even noticed me as she squeezed past, so focused was she on pushing through to the next level of the sieve. Others gave her measured encouragement. Jasmine was a seasoned athlete and way beyond a shallow, rah-rah approach. In my opinion, there was a good chance that if anyone had tried to give her a smiley face kind of pat on the back, she would have used those weight-lifting arms to rip their head off.

Jasmine eventually disappeared from my sight, making her way to the next level. I could hear her breathing long after I could no longer see her. Thirty minutes later, I watched as she navigated a tightrope 100 feet in the air, in the rain. Every muscle shaking—from fear and the instability of the cable—she made her deliberate sidestepping way to the next platform. I studied her face. It was obvious she was pulling on everything she'd learned as a professional athlete—focus, determination, tenacity, courage. When she got to the other side and was "safely" atop a platform not much bigger than her behind, she clapped her hands in glee and then folded them in prayer. And cried.

It was gut-wrenching to watch. I knew so well what she was enduring, the real, definitive terror she was feeling. To make matters worse, she'd made it through the sieve and across the tightrope only to have to face the scariest obstacle of all. The only way down was the "Big Swing," where—still harnessed—she had to slide/jump off the platform into a sort of free fall, evoking images of those land divers on Pentecost Island in the South Pacific who jump to prove their manhood, only Jasmine had a much better safety system in place.

Jasmine was hooked in to the swing mechanism, and I watched while the instructor spoke close to her ear. Whether it was encouragement or instructions, I wasn't sure, but I saw something I hadn't seen before. Just the tiniest slump in her shoulders. Was she giving up? Would she be able to pull it all together for the most important leap of all?

Jasmine sat on the platform and held the rope with both hands. I could tell she was praying. I also recognized that moment of internal disintegration, where she was finding some way to pull everything that had unraveled inside of her back into a nice, tight ball. One deep, focusing breath later, she jumped. I felt myself go with her.

The crowd of people below and the 15 participants on the ropes course screamed like wild animals as Jasmine swung through the air, back and forth like a giant pendulum. She released her grip on the rope to spread both arms out beside her, like new wings unfurling in the drizzly light.

The next day Jasmine stood in front of the group and informed us she had buried the person that had been holding her back for so long.

"I've made a commitment," she said, "to keeping that person buried. Her ghost will *not* haunt me anymore."

Since I had seen Jasmine's transformation with my own eyes, I asked her a week later if she'd mind talking to me about it.

Jasmine's backstory is of a 16-year-old who loved volleyball but got talked into trying out for Olympic weight lifting. People, she said, always saw potential in her that she didn't see in herself. Successful in sports, Jasmine placed sixth in the state of California in her Olympic weight-lifting class. She extended her last year in college to study Spanish, living in Costa Rica. But she had a fear that dogged her all the way along a path where every signpost should have pointed to her success. She was terrified she'd repeat her mother's mistake of falling for the wrong men and being forced to live a difficult life—single mom to a daughter fathered by a crack addict, with all the heartache, betrayal, suffering, and toil that brings. And despite her fear, that's exactly where Jasmine's early road ended. She attended law school but dropped out and found herself pregnant a year and a half later. She also found that she had married a "functional" addict, whose crack addiction had been well hidden. He burned through their money, and when both of them went to live with Jasmine's mother, it was with a promise of a new, clean, fresh start. But the pull of drugs was stronger than the pull of a responsible life. Jasmine eventually divorced him and raised her daughter on her own.

"I had to put my dreams in a hidden place for a long time," she said. "I worked three jobs to support my daughter and went on public assistance. My life felt like it was spiraling out of control."

What helped turn Jasmine around was the introspection she'd engaged in for most of her young life. As an only child, she'd had a lot of time to think. Practicing the sport of weight lifting taught her the discipline of being in "a zone." Later, while studying abroad, travel gave her time to ask important questions, the big "What now?" At 23 years old, Jasmine figured out what was in her core and that the few things that really mattered to her were love, family, and health.

Ten years later, at 33, those things haven't changed, and now she also includes faith. Yet, despite embracing those positive tenets, Jasmine was dogged by something lurking inside, an alter ego, the Jasmine who blocked potential, who convinced the other Jasmine she was limited in her abilities, who conspired with fear and welcomed its destructive power.

"In the sieve," Jasmine told me, referring back to that day on the ropes course, "every insecurity I ever had spilled out. It was terror. I felt like I was being made to pay for all my sins. Here I was being forced to climb an unstable, medieval tower. It was such a metaphor. I mean, who *doesn't* want stability?"

"What kept you going?" I asked.

"I wasn't going to punk out," she said, the determination of the Olympic weight lifter animating her face. "That tower wasn't going to beat me." The tipping point, Jasmine told me, was the second platform on the sieve, when she asked herself, *How am I going to do this?* It was then, she said, that she had to take herself out of her head. She pulled on everything she'd ever used in her life: her intense focus from weight lifting, her breathing technique from yoga, the trick she'd learned to convince the body that it wasn't feeling pain. "At every platform I had to leave a little bit of myself behind. As I did, I felt a little less fear because I was closer to my goal. I thought about something my grandmother once asked me: 'How do you eat an elephant?' So I started talking to myself, telling myself to 'place your foot here.' It was one bite at a time."

At each platform Jasmine took a moment to ground herself and recognize the accomplishment she'd just made. At the top, before crossing the tightwire, she asked one of the instructors for permission to cry. "And then it just all came out. I had to release that stress and anxiety before I went any farther." As she readied herself for the tightwire walk, people touched her, spoke to her. One man put his hands on her shoulders and she said it felt like she was being protected by "a wall." She gathered all that strength from strangers, and took it with her into her zone.

Crossing the tightwire, step by shaky step, Jasmine never looked down. Instead, she spied a leaf at the very top of the highest tree in the forest surrounding the tower. Waving in the breeze, it was almost as if, in its tiny way, the leaf was encouraging her to continue. She never took her eyes off it.

The jump and swing at the end were ultimately a symbol for what Jasmine was abandoning. Already, she'd left a little bit of her old self and a lot of her negativity on every platform she conquered. When she jumped into thin air, the distance between her new self and the old one was too big to bridge. She'd finally broken free.

The next morning she visited the outdoor chapel on the retreat grounds and conducted a funeral for her former self. "When I finished the eulogy," she told me, "a huge gust of wind came out of nowhere and blew so strong, even though the morning was calm." This was further confirmation, Jasmine said, that her old self was really gone, dead and buried. Jasmine was free to begin walking the path to a new life.

And that's Jasmine's commitment. Her old self will stay buried in the soil of her past. "Proclaiming it and doing it," she said, "is the promise I've made to myself. I now know the greatness is in me. How will I get there? The same way I crossed the wire: a step at a time."

Jasmine admitted that before coming to the leadership retreat, she'd done a lot of preliminary work to get herself into a place where she could be receptive to growth. That included practicing yoga, reviving her weight-lifting routine, and reading personal development books. Although she was ready to live in a new way, she didn't know how to rid herself of the bad Jasmine. The ropes course left her no choice—it tore her in two, which was painful and terrifying at the time, but ultimately, it was the very thing needed in order for her to assert her one, authentic self. The ordeal on the wire forced a metamorphosis she still might be seeking if she hadn't challenged herself in such a profound way.

"I feel like a big burden has been lifted," she told me, "carried away by the wind. The little things don't agitate me anymore. I can more easily go back to my inner resource and pull it closer to my heart. It opened up that ugly place inside of me to an open, airy space that can now receive love."

I thanked Jasmine for her candor, and for her inspiration that day in the rain. The last thing she quoted on her way out the door was from Marianne Williamson's *A Return to Love: Reflections on the Principles of 'A Course in Miracles'*: "A miracle is a change in perception."

A week after interviewing Jasmine, as this book deadline was bearing down on me, I needed to take a break to sort out my jumbled thoughts and shake off some of the stress that was blocking the writing. I didn't have time for a long hike, so I went to the Daniel Stowe Botanical Garden, 15 minutes away from my home in Gastonia, North Carolina. I hadn't visited there all spring or summer and knew the time for enjoying blooms was fading fast. Once there, I learned that a butterfly exhibit had recently opened and that the "caterpillar frames" had just been set out. Butterflies are nice, but all I was really looking for was some quiet time in nature, so I didn't pay much attention to anything the attendant was telling me. She secured the admission bracelet on my wrist and off I went to wind my way through the various gardens, noting the abundance of dragonflies, bees, and, yes, hundreds and hundreds of butterflies.

Throughout the gardens, fountains spewed white foamy water in all variations of form and cadence. Hypnotic. Snippets of my conversation with Jasmine kept playing in my head. An epiphany was trying to worm its way out from under the pile of ideas I'd unintentionally stacked upon it. At the orchid conservatory—a glass cathedral with waterfalls and grottoes—I came across one of the caterpillar frames. Really just a television-size aquarium with a latching door, it held dozens of different species of cocoons tacked to horizontal bars, so that viewers on the outside could watch the various stages of metamorphosis. At the very moment I gazed through the glass, one orange butterfly scurried along the floor of the frame, slowly opening and closing its perfect wings. Another lay on the floor, its wings crumpled and useless. Why would it be dead already, I wondered? At the same time, a yellow butterfly was making its way out into the world, pushing with all its might to get free of its cocoon. The "dead" butterfly on the floor waggled its antennae and moved its wings a little. I watched with total fascination as bit by bit the wings lost their creases and took on their true shape. The butterfly breathed heavily but waited patiently for the moment when it could begin its new life, no longer a creature that destroys plants but one that ensures their survival.

Next to the caterpillar frame was an interpretive sign listing a few interesting facts about butterflies. While in the cocoon, the pupa has to liquefy before it can transform into a butterfly; scientists aren't really sure why. I smiled: here was another one of nature's unfathomable mysteries, not meant for us to know but simply to ponder in amazement. And there was the epiphany: *No transformation comes from a place of comfort.* Sometimes, everything has to dissolve before something new can be resurrected. Hadn't I learned this in the Utah canyons? Hadn't I just seen it happen with Jasmine's courageous leap? No meaningful change happens just because you want it to. In order to move from one reality to the next, you have to be willing to take risks wherever you find them in life—and sometimes you have to go looking for them. There are the kinds of risk that really unnerve you, that shake you to your core and make you wonder what you're made of, that melt you like iron ore and then hammer you into something new; the kinds of tests you can't study for. But they don't all have to be tests on the edge, across a tightrope or in a canyon.

They can be quiet ones that are just as risky—starting your own business, forgiving someone who has hurt you, quitting your job to travel the globe—and these are just as rewarding when the test is finally taken and passed.

The good news is that we don't have to wait for life to throw that test our way before we figure out the answers. Challenging ourselves helps us commit to a new way of living, to finding out who we are at various stages and places in our lives. Every challenge will be unique to the person who rises to it, but it has to be meaningful and throw you into completely uncharted territory.

It's a journey, a journey that will be accelerated if you shed your excess baggage. Get rid of the clutter, the emotional burdens, entanglements, all the accumulated junk. Just like any other trip, it will unravel more smoothly if you travel light and only pack what you can carry. When I go into the canyons, I take a rope, my gear, and little else. Jasmine took nothing with her on the swing but her resolve. Terry ran with his artificial leg and the clothes on his back. The caterpillar takes nothing with it on its journey to change except a surrender to its instincts. Transformation doesn't require any gear or gadgets; it simply requires you.

Committing to challenge yourself for the rest of your life means you will always know how to find yourself when you're lost, how to grow when you're stagnant, how to get out of the cocoon of your safe and bundled-up life and transform into something delicate and beautiful. As I watched the butterfly's wings slowly unfold, I thought of Jasmine on the swing, how she suddenly burst free of her self-made cocoon, spread her wings, and—for one extraordinary moment—found she could fly.

EXERCISES

WHY COMMITMENT?

Building solitude into your life, for the rest of your life, means you will always have time for meaningful introspection. When you're able to think deeply and clearly about your life's path, you'll identify obstacles long before they stall your progress. Tackling those obstacles when they present themselves will build your capacity for courage, which means that during your whole life, you can continue moving forward, even when everything conspires to make you stop. Committing to this process means you're committing to creating and re-creating the life you want, for the rest of your life.

EXERCISES IN COMMITMENT

Create a Timeline

Draw a horizontal line on a piece of paper. Mark where you are now and mark a spot near the edge of the page to indicate an end point: retirement, expected life span, graduation—whatever conclusion you want to envision. Between that point and where you are now, mark the milestones you hope to achieve. Do you want to train for a triathlon? Go back to school? Pay off your mortgage? If so, when, and what steps will need to happen in between? Mapping it like this will help you create a precise plan and identify what you'll be willing to sacrifice—you may have to make an enormous lifestyle shift, but it will be much easier to give up daily indulgences when you can see on paper how it will pay off in the end. Creating a timeline on paper makes the unknown less scary and more manageable, and allows you to plan your destiny as opposed to simply reacting to whatever comes at you. By making a timeline for your life, you can commit to staying the course.

Take a Fresh Look Around

Part of committing to the process is giving yourself new experiences. I like to do it with adventure trips where I'm forced to step out of my comfort zone, and most likely there are plenty of similar opportunities within a 50-mile radius of where you are now. Take a map of your area (leave the GPS for later), lay it out on a table, and look at where you live. Search around your location for pockets of green and blue—parks and lakes—as well as where wide-open spaces and densely bunched urban areas lie. Within a 50-mile radius, how much of this area have you explored? Identify all the places in your own backyard you've never visited, decide which ones interest you, and commit to visiting one new place every month or so. Your own chamber of commerce has lots of information designed to lure tourists to your area, so take a look to see what they're touting. Who knows what you'll find out about your hometown and what's going on there.

Make a "Bucket List"

What are the four or five things you want to make sure you do before you die? For one of my friends, it's to be able to ski 30 days each year. For another, it's to visit every country in the world. For yet another, it's to make peace with every member in her estranged family. There will be financial and/or emotional costs attached to the items on your list, so commit now to cache the resources necessary to achieve these goals.

EXERCISES TOWARD ONLY PACKING WHAT YOU CAN CARRY

Commit to Packing Light
Commit to slowly and deliberately shedding excess baggage for the rest of your life. You don't need half the things you think you do. De-clutter your mind and your living space. Learn how to make sacrifices. When you can commit to only packing what you can carry, life becomes easily navigable. With your hands free to grab at life, you can pull important experiences, memories, and learning into your stash of knowledge. This is the road that will eventually lead you to wisdom. And peace.

Say Yes
Through solitude you learned to "notice." You paid attention to how you felt during different parts of the day and in different situations. Notice how you feel when you're presented with the opportunity to do something new, something different, something scary. Pay attention to your impulse to say no, and say yes instead. Take a chance—take many chances. The filmmaker and philosopher Arnaud Desjardins said it best: "You cannot live sheltered forever without ever being exposed, and at the same time be a spiritual adventurer. Be audacious. Be crazy in your own way . . . take risks, search and search again, search everywhere, in every way, do not let a single opportunity or chance that life offers pass you by."

CHAPTER SIX

ONLY PACK WHAT YOU CAN CARRY

Saying yes instead of no requires its own kind of courage. It requires acknowledging that the unknown, though scary, might just lead to something great.

WRITING THIS BOOK HAS BEEN a different kind of journey, more interior but just as revealing as my first descent into the canyons. Until I'd written the introduction, I'd forgotten about the scars hacked into my psyche by the grown-up world, how in my ten-year-old outrage I built a wall to protect myself from harm, to separate from vulnerability, to maintain a sense of safety and to keep everyone and everything at arm's length. It served its purpose: I *did* protect myself from those whose intentions were suspect, but eventually, that wall changed from ally to enemy, the fortress keeping things out but locking me in as well. Later, when life asked that I be vulnerable, I didn't know how to respond. I'd built my wall to last and mortared it so expertly that there was nowhere to chisel out an escape hatch.

Decades passed while I tried to deconstruct that wall, brick by painstaking brick, until life did it for me with a series of sledgehammer blows: a serious illness; a horrible riding accident; a postsurgical complication that almost killed me; the devastating events of September 11, 2001, which I took as personally as if I'd been there; the loss of a career. All these trials spanned a five-year period, forcing an unprecedented, ruthless examination of my life. I knew I didn't want to live in that walled-up place anymore. I just didn't know how to get out.

The way I escaped was something so straightforward I didn't recognize its power at the time. It was simply exchanging an impulse to say no for one that said yes. The 2004 trip to Costa Rica—where I had the big "aha" moment on horseback and the photograph of me galloping on the white horse through the blue surf became the new advertisement for the ride—was a perfect example. In spite of its fantastic outcome (and one of the most enjoyable vacations of my life), the entrée to that trip was awful. Six weeks before departure date, I broke my toe, making it impossible to wear a riding boot and erasing any opportunity to physically train for the hours and hours I would spend in the saddle. The government "misplaced" my passport renewal; I still didn't have a passport the day before I was due to leave. The initial flight out was aborted during takeoff due to failed engine hydraulics, and by the time we shifted to another plane, I missed my connection in Miami. The airline representative asked if I wanted to take the flight to San José and then a six-hour taxicab ride to the hotel, or if I wanted to wait until morning to catch the next flight to Liberia, my intended destination and the city closest to the resort where I'd be staying.

"You have one minute to decide," the representative said, as I looked over her shoulder at the armed guards and drug-sniffing dogs standing sentry at the entrance to the airplane.

"I don't have any choice," I answered. "Tomorrow everyone leaves on horseback. If I wait, I won't know where they are."

"Well?" She glared.

The word that formed in my head was "no": I had travel insurance, and this was a covered event. If I backed out now, I wouldn't lose a dime and I could put an end to all the months of stress I'd endured just trying to *prepare* for the trip. How many bad omens would it take to convince me that this trip was doomed?

The rep was waiting for an answer. "No" is what I planned to say, but what came out of my mouth was "yes." I was immediately whisked past the guards and the dogs and onto the flight that had been held just for me. Thirty minutes airborne, I suddenly realized that there was no way my luggage could have made it. I'd be arriving at my riding vacation without boots, jodhpurs, underwear . . . not even a bathing suit!

In San José, an airline employee was ready to pay for a taxi to take me to my hotel in the Guanacaste region on the west coast, but on the World Health Organization website, prior to leaving Charlotte, I'd read about a recent rash of assaults against women traveling alone—by cabdrivers in San José.

"I'm afraid," I confessed to the airline rep, after he said something to the driver in Spanish and handed him some official-looking papers.

"Well, you don't have to go," he said. "I can see you're uncomfortable, but if it's any consolation, I'd put my own mother in this cab and feel OK about it."

"Does he speak any English?" I whispered, nodding my head in the direction of the driver.

"Not a word." The rep smiled. "Have a good vacation."

On the long, quiet drive to Sugar Beach, I persuaded the driver to let me use his cell phone—mine wouldn't work in Costa Rica, it turned out, unless I bought a special, government-controlled "chip." I dialed the local contact number provided by the travel company, hoping to get help with my luggage predicament. The woman who answered on the other end was apologetic.

"I'm sorry," she said, "I used to be the vendor for that travel company but they changed last week. I can't help you."

Frustration bubbled inside of me like pressure inside a volcano, and suddenly I vented—a little too creatively. Chinese ribbons danced around in the front of the taxicab as the driver peeled down the bumpy road.

"Listen," said the woman on the other end, "I'll call the hotel and tell them what happened. They'll know who to contact. And if you tell me what size shoe and what size riding pants you wear, I'll see if I can get some clothes together for you. I'll meet you at the hotel in five hours." She paused. "And don't worry."

"Thank you," I said, and hung up. I hoped she'd be true to her word. In the cab the silence, which was awkward to begin with, was even more clunky now that it had been broken by a jarring cell phone conversation. I decided the best thing to do was go to sleep. If I was going to be attacked, I'd be attacked whether I was lucid or dreaming, so I opted for the latter.

When we arrived at Sugar Beach, six hours later, the proprietor said he didn't have a room for me and he didn't know what I was talking about when I asked what time the group dinner was.

"There's a group dinner," I explained slowly, glaring at him, my last nerve about to explode into shards, "where the riders are supposed to meet the guide. What time will that be?"

"Nine o'clock," he answered.

"Nine? Are you sure?"

"Seven."

"Seven? Are you making this up?"

"Six," he said, smiling. "Yes, five o'clock."

After much sighing and shuffling of papers, he "found" a room and handed me the key. I snatched it from him and stormed off, deciding right then and there that this trip was going to be over before it began. If this welcome was any indication of what was to come, better I bail out now rather than open myself up for more disappointment later. I couldn't endure another cab ride right away, but after a good night's sleep I'd be leaving.

Without luggage, a journal, or even a pencil to stab myself with, I decided to take a walk on the beach. But a knock at the door quashed that plan.

"Now what?" I muttered as I opened the door to a small-framed, blond, tanned woman in her 40s. She looked awfully familiar.

"Hi," she said, reaching out her hand to shake mine. "We talked on the phone earlier. I have some riding clothes for you."

I waved her inside and she laid the tattered but useful treasures on the bed. I couldn't stop staring. I knew I'd met her before.

And then it dawned on me. She was the woman in the pictures I'd seen all those years ago, the blond woman on the white horse galloping in the white surf of a Costa Rican beach. And just like that, my no turned to yes, and the rest, as they say, is history.

There would be more "yes" moments after Costa Rica, and evidence of another important one is the book you now hold in your hands. After I learned of the elimination of my job with the Girl Scouts in 2009, I decided to go to Canada for a while to visit my family and then attend a monthlong writer's workshop at the Banff Centre, the very place I'd started *really* writing, 26 years earlier. I had signed up for the workshop while I was still employed and had an income, but as termination day inched closer, I began to think about finances and wondered if I really wanted to pay all that money just for a quiet place to write.

I knew the program had a waiting list, and more than once I began to write the e-mail that said, "Due to limited financial resources, I sadly decline the offer to attend." I'd write that e-mail, walk away, come back, hover over the send button, and then press delete. Yet every time I tried to say no, yes came out instead.

The first week I was there, the Banff Mountain Film and Book Festivals were under way. One of the sponsors was National Geographic. It was there that I met Barbara Brownell Grogan, the editor in chief of the National Geographic Book Division. She showed an interest in my work and in the idea for this book. Our preliminary conversations at Banff led to telephone conversations and e-mail exchanges and ultimately an offer of publication. A year later, I handed in the final chapters for *Only Pack What You Can Carry*. You would not be reading this book if I'd succumbed to my worries over finances, if I'd said no instead of yes.

Saying yes instead of no requires its own kind of courage. It requires acknowledging that although scary, the unknown might just lead to something great. The fact that it might also lead to something else is what makes the choice to take action definitively courageous. Saying yes instead of no is something that everyone, everywhere, at any level of education, income, status, age, or circumstance, can do to unlock the door to new potential. It has certainly worked for me.

Arriving now at the end of this book, I am thinking about how it all began with solo travel; how when I first set out alone there were so many people—people who genuinely loved me—trying to talk me out of it. It was too risky, they insisted, too dangerous. Their fear was not so much that I would be injured, or that I'd get lost, but that I might *die*.

For more than a decade I've thought about that; in fact, I think about it every time I plan a risky adventure. *Might this kill me?* I ask myself, *and if it does, will I be OK with that?*

Here's my answer: Better to die in a beautiful canyon or atop a majestic mountain or surfing a monstrous, curling wave than to succumb to disease, an inattentive driver, or a plane crash. Philippe Petit, before he walked a tightrope between the two towers of the Word Trade Center, acknowledged that this boldest of stunts might be his last.

"If I die," he said, smiling, "what a beautiful death!"

Twice I have faced death because of illness, but in more than ten years of solo adventures I've had only a few moments when I really thought I might die. In Utah, having to rely on that Munter hitch to save me from falling down a waterfall was one of them. And there was another time, when I took what I thought was a calculated risk and found myself in what easily could have turned out to be the wrong place at the wrong time.

The Virgin River has carved some of most spectacular canyon formations in Zion National Park, and one of my all-time favorite hikes, which takes place almost entirely in the river, is through the Narrows. Typically, it's a well-traveled route, at least at the onset, where the river is fairly wide and shallow, and visitors can walk an easy, paved path to get there. But the water is always bone-chillingly cold, and the upstream going is tiring, especially in footwear not designed to navigate submerged rocks. The attrition rate is about 60 percent; if you can endure the crowds for the first half hour, your reward is a sparsely populated walk through thousand-foot-high chocolate- and caramel-colored sandstone walls, a pre-historic spectacle of stone and water and mystery.

On one visit to Utah, I saved the Narrows for my last day—I wanted a spectacular end to another memorable trip. As I rode the park shuttle to the Temple of Sinawava and the mile-long paved trail that would lead me to the river, it began to rain. The big danger in the Narrows is the same as in every other slot canyon: flash flooding. It's not a good idea to enter a canyon when it's actively raining, so one should always check the weather forecast for the general area. It can be sunny and dry in one location, but a thunderstorm 50 miles away can dump so much water that a flash flood is almost inevitable.

"Do you know the forecast?" I asked the shuttle driver as I departed.

"Light rain, all day," she answered. I walked the easy path and 15 minutes later arrived at the entrance to the Narrows hike, the canyon opening up to welcome visitors, the water shallow, frigid, and clear.

As usual, there was a crowd of people, some splashing around at the edge of the river, some sitting on rocks, a few in bare feet attempting to hike but realizing quickly that the freezing water and algae-covered rocks below the swiftly moving current were not going to be easily navigated. Twenty people were upstream at various stages of progress, some holding walking sticks and moving with purpose, others shivering and pausing, uncertain whether to continue.

Light rain, all day.

Should I do it?

The voice in my head said no. There was no fear lurking amid the boulders of the Narrows, but I knew that once far enough inside, where the sandstone walls reached 2,000 sheer feet, there would be no escape if a torrent of water smashed through the canyon. I hesitated for a very long time before taking my first steps into the icy water. I'd be leaving Utah late that afternoon, so this was my one and only chance to hike the hike I loved so much. I made a compromise: walk for a while and see what happens. I could always turn back.

Even with just a light rain, the current was stronger than usual and I fell early on, cutting my knee and twisting my ankle a little. Everyone in front of, behind, and next to me was also struggling. I stayed focused on the water, the rocks beneath the surface, and where I was putting my feet. I didn't notice at first that 30 minutes later everyone else had turned back. *Did they know something I didn't?* An hour into the hike I was utterly alone. The whole magnificent place was mine to enjoy. That little voice in my head admonished me to turn around. I ignored it—when would I ever have this experience again, with just myself and the million-plus years of geologic sculpture towering on either side of me?

Two hours into the hike I arrived at Orderville Canyon, cutting its own distinctive path into the massive walls on the right.

There are a couple little waterfalls where Orderville meets the Virgin River, so I hiked in, to see if they were pushing more water than usual. They were.

Orderville Canyon marks the place in the Narrows where the canyon begins to squeeze in on you—sometimes only 20 to 30 feet wide—and where the scenery becomes epic. It's a natural turnaround spot for many hikers; they're tired from fighting the current, cold from the water, and they've got at least another hour and a half on the return, making an almost four-hour hike roundtrip in challenging conditions.

Go back or press on? Against my better judgment, I continued upstream, knowing that the best scenery was about to come. Almost immediately the canyon constricted, becoming darker and much, much cooler. A raven flew through the narrow corridor. I saw it cock its head to look at me. Five minutes later it returned and sat on a rock, watching. Every time I turned a corner it followed, finding some dry place to sit and observe. At first I fancied that the raven, also alone, was entertaining itself, perhaps hoping I'd stop somewhere for lunch and toss it a morsel or two. But then I remembered that in some Native American cultures, the raven is a messenger of death.

And then I heard it—a deep, rumbling noise, not thunder, because it wasn't overhead. The sound was in the canyon and it was getting closer. One of the harbingers of a flash flood is the sound—a great booming as the crazed water makes its violent, churning way through the twists and turns of the narrow canyon.

This was it. In moments I would be overtaken by water and debris. A huge, waterborne tree would knock me unconscious and I'd be smashed to smithereens, my bones tinkling like crushed glass inside my skin as the water tumbled me along on its wild journey. There was only one way to save myself, and that was to get to higher ground. But I was in the steepest part of the canyon; behind me were just sheer walls, so I hurried ahead to the next turn—maybe, with any luck, I'd find a boulder to scramble onto. As I stumbled over rocks, I took my last good look around.

The roar of water was undeniable, and it seemed I was about to become part of the canyons I loved so much. By the time the flood was done with me, I'd be ground into layers of sediment that would eventually harden into rock. I was going to end my days here, alone, in this magnificent canyon. But I wasn't sad and I wasn't afraid. Of all the places I could die, I knew then with certainty, this is the one I would choose.

The booming was now almost deafening. The water level had risen by several inches, but strangely, it was still clear. In a flash flood, before the killing wave of water appears, the river water will turn muddy, sending clogs of debris as a warning. Except for the swiftness of the current, the water looked the same as when I started, clear and bright. Turning the corner, I braced myself. The crashing sound was right next to me but there was no wave, no wall of water approaching. I stood for a moment, confused.

The sound was coming from *inside* the canyon walls.

What? I wondered, placing my ear against a slab of wet, black rock. Behind that inscrutable facade was another world, hidden from my view, a world where waterfalls fell into blackness, fed by rain and snowmelt, carving the inside of the canyon into hoodoo shapes that would never see the light of day.

A raging waterfall inside a rock.

I'd hiked this canyon many times, but never in the rain.

Precipitation was swelling not just the Virgin River but the rivulets at the top of the canyon that feed into the cracks and fissures of the stone walls. It made sense that the rain above had to go somewhere. Yes, there was a flash flood, but it was pummeling into whatever secret river wound through that dark, interior place behind the black rock beside me.

Just ahead, a large boulder provided a place to sit and eat some food. I offered the raven a piece of bread, as thanks for watching over me, but it didn't take my offering. It simply sat and watched until I put my feet in the water and headed back downstream. Then it ruffled its feathers and flew away, down-canyon, disappearing against a backdrop of dark rock.

On the exhausting hike back, I had several hours wading through cold water, in the tight, sunless labyrinth of stone, to think about what had just happened. I'd believed I was about to be killed in a flash flood, and the one thought—the only thought—I had was that I was grateful to be in a place of beauty, the place that had animated my dreams for so long, a place I loved with more than just my heart. What a loss it would have been if I'd never taken that first solo trip to southern Utah, the one that eventually opened all the doors fear had closed, and, in time, brought me to this unforgettable place.

I thought about Amelia Earhart, the first woman to fly solo nonstop across the Atlantic Ocean, in 1932. She disappeared in 1937 during her round-the-world flight, but she was doing what she loved. People would ask Amelia about the risks: "Obviously I faced the possibility of not returning when first I considered going. Once faced and settled there really wasn't any good reason to refer to it. The most difficult thing is the decision to act, the rest is merely tenacity. The fears are paper tigers. You can do anything you decide to do. You can act to change and control your life; and the procedure, the process is its own reward. . . . Flying may not be all plain sailing, but the fun of it is worth the price."

If the price of doing what you love is that you might die doing it, what is the price of *not* chasing your dreams or fulfilling your potential? The cost is an interior death, where your dreams, ideas, hopes, and schemes wither away, leaving a hollow core to be filled with superficial distractions or worse, with nothing. Filmmaker and spiritualist Arnaud Desjardins has so many wonderful thoughts on this subject. One of my favorites is this proclamation: "Daring to live means daring to die at any moment but also means daring to be born, crossing great stages of life in which the person we have been dies and is replaced with another with a renewed vision of the world, and at the same time realizing that there will be many obstacles to overcome."

Daring to be born. What an invitation to embrace life, even when it means, as Desjardins reminds us, that the person we are now will have to die in order to become something new. Just as the butterfly cannot become a winged beauty until its pupa liquefies in the cocoon, we can't be transformed until our former self is laid to rest.

Desjardins's statement about crossing great stages of life to discover a renewed vision of the world brings me back to my mother, Katie, who wanted to shed her labels so she could discover her true self. Long before that morning when we talked over breakfast about how she was trying to discover who she was in her head and in her heart, she had endured years of chronic, undiagnosed pain. Her discomfort and dissatisfaction forced her into a self-imposed solitude. Being around people got to be too much work, she'd convinced herself, because she was tired of always having to explain being tired. The solitude led her to a long, extended period of introspection where she was able to create a routine: journal writing during breakfast, then a brisk walk through the woods near her house in Sidney, British Columbia. I'd shared that walk with her once, and she'd showed me the trees that had become her friends. She knew how they grew and changed with the seasons, and they were always there on her morning walks, watching over her.

"Oh, my friend," she said, hugging one of the trees, "you never let me down."

I noticed that in the woods, my mother's gait seemed easier; I had to walk quickly to keep up. In the woods she smiled more and seemed content. Back in the house, she was more likely to focus on her pain, her confusion, and dissatisfaction. Being in nature throughout her period of introspection led Katie finally to her biggest epiphany, the one that turned everything upside down and allowed her to see reality in a new way.

She'd been out walking along the harbor in Sidney, on a crisp and vivid fall day. With no rain or fog to obscure it, Mount Baker in neighboring Washington State formed a majestic backdrop to the green harbor waters and the azure blue sky. Feeling a draw she couldn't really explain, Katie walked the length of the pier to a dock, overlooking the water and backdropped by the ancient volcano that is Mount Baker. Hands on hips, she raised her face to the sun. With eyes closed, she turned slowly in a circle, breathing in the air, listening to the seagulls fighting over scraps from the fish market just a stone's throw away. When she opened her eyes, Katie knew something she hadn't known before that moment, that "everything is the way it's supposed to be."

At the very same time Katie was acknowledging this new insight, a newspaper photographer was snapping her photo, the shot newsworthy because of the fantastic and rare view of Mount Baker. The picture was printed on the front page of the newspaper the next day. When I look at it, I can tell that the photographer captured more than just a natural wonder, she captured a pivotal moment in a person's life.

"I felt such peace," Katie told me. "I knew then that if I hadn't suffered all these years, I might never have woken up. I might never have taken the time to really find out who I am inside." She paused for a moment. "And as hard as it is for a mother to let go, I have to let my kids make their own mistakes. I have to let them suffer, if that's what it takes for them to learn."

Recently, Katie decided to attend her 60th college reunion after hemming and hawing about it for months. She didn't want to travel because she didn't want to sit on an airplane and be miserable. "But you'll be sitting at home being miserable, so what's the difference?" my brother Rob said. "So go and be miserable there and maybe you'll have some fun."

Katie said yes instead of no and her life changed. While there, she reunited with a man she'd met at her 25th reunion. They had become soul mates then, and now he was widowed. He and Katie were free to explore a new kind of friendship that would sustain them through their later years. Having spent a long time thinking about the life she wanted, Katie is now able to make her next decision based not on infatuation or repeating the lines of an old, outdated script, but on a foundation of understanding who she is and what will content her in the last years of her life.

Katie, finally, has found her compass.

And what of my divorced friend, the one who embraced suffering as a way to find healing and peace after his divorce? Checking in with him nearly three years after our first conversation about suffering, I found him to be not just content—which is about all he'd hoped for back then—but really, deeply happy. It's not that he hasn't had his trials either: the untimely death of a loved one, financial struggles. I was impressed that he'd accomplished most of the emotional goals he'd set for himself and was enjoying more of the things that fulfilled him. Bit by bit, he was shedding the baggage of obligations to others, obligations that *didn't* fulfill him. "So," I asked him, "did you consciously commit to make the change?"

"I'm not sure I thought about it in those terms," he said, after thinking for a minute. "It really was a matter of just *starting*. It's like when you finally decide to lose weight. You try and you try and you go back and forth, but then you just get sick and tired of being fat. It's that place inside where you just aren't willing to accept your state anymore, and that's when you're able to make a *real* pledge to lose weight. You have to get to the point where you know that going back to where you were just isn't an option anymore. But the key is starting. That's all I did. I just took the first step."

On the day I wrote the final sentences of this epilogue, I rode my horse Brazen through the scary woods, on a day so alive with color and sound, no painter could have captured it more perfectly. On a mile-long path of grass, with woods and a stream flanking one side and thickets of thorny blackberry, wild rosebushes, and yellow daisies on the other, we cantered along, spooking birds from the bushes, dodging squirrels and snakes all along the way. Brazen's gait was cadenced and relaxed, even when a rabbit

darted in between his front feet. There was no wild-eyed rushing, no snorting or head tossing, no hauling back on the reins to
keep him in check.

I thought back to the years of struggling to repair from that
horrific riding accident and how we would end our outings in the
woods in misery—me in tears, Brazen a foaming mass of nerves.
Every rustle in the bushes, every creak of a tree limb was like an
electric shock to both of us. In retrospect, it was everything post-
traumatic stress is cracked up to be. Even as the years passed and
we had no further incidents, fear still lurked in the shadows, not
just ruining our rides but diminishing my enthusiasm for riding
in general.

Finally, I just couldn't do it anymore. I couldn't take the hours
of being on high alert, of not knowing if I'd come back from a ride
astride my horse or lying prone in an ambulance. I decided to sell
Brazen. Deep inside, I feared it was just a matter of time before
the next mishap, one that would kill me. How long would it take
before I'd admit that Brazen and I together were never going to
get over the accident? Maybe he needed a different rider and I
needed another horse. But it wasn't that easy to let him go. The
night before I planned to accept an offer for purchase, I called
off the deal. I didn't know how I was going to salve the wound
of our accident, but I knew if I sold him, a scar would form over
any chance to recover my former joy of riding.

And there was something else, too. I'd had Brazen since he was
born. He was my last connection to the greatest horse I'd ever
owned, the stallion Lover's Reason. When Brazen came into the
world on a snowy, April morning in Buffalo, New York, he was
almost a month premature and small enough that I could hold

him in my arms. His innocence and sweetness, his entertaining antics as a foal, got me through the dark days of my divorce and distracted me from the worries of a dwindling income. Brazen was his nickname because he didn't seem to be afraid of anything. Before he was old enough to ride, we'd go for long walks together, through the woods, down busy roads, we'd even swim in ponds.

As he grew into a big-boned, powerful Thoroughbred, I had dreams of his becoming a really good event horse—a horse versatile enough to do the intricate patterns of dressage, jump fences cross-country through fields, and at the end of it all, accurately navigate a stadium course of jumps—and dreams of my becoming a really good event rider. All the horses I'd had before Brazen were too damaged or lacked the necessary talent to excel in all three areas. But Brazen had talent enough for ten horses. And he had an attitude of willingness and curiosity that meant he'd approach his work enthusiastically. Our accident changed everything: It broke my bones, Brazen's confidence, and any dream I ever had of galloping unscathed through the countryside.

Yet here we were now, more than ten years later, galloping in the grass, under the late summer sunshine, blue sky overhead, birds circling and filling the air with incessant chatter. How remarkable, after all these years of struggle, unable to communicate through language, so frustrated with each other, so willing to succumb to fear, that we made it through to the other side, *together*.

I did it through perseverance, through trying to build my courage in other ways, through talking it out with coaches and trainers. Brazen had to figure out a way to do it on his own, without the benefit of counseling or other supports. He had to do it the way we all have to do it—just suck it up and move on. His ability to recover from our accident inspires me every time I feel fear. *If Brazen could do it,* I tell myself, *I have no excuse worth speaking of.*

What a tragedy it would have been to have sold him, never to have won the reward of this day, to have quietly declared defeat and acquiesced to a memory. A part of me would have died inside, strangled quickly by the fast-growing vines of regret. I thought a lot about what my divorced friend said about starting. For more than ten years I felt like I was starting over every time I dared to put my foot in the stirrup and swing my leg across Brazen's back. To say *yes, I will ride you.* Every single time the energy it took to *start* was more than the energy it took for the whole ride. When did it turn, I wondered? When did I stop fretting about dying and really start living again?

I think a lot about something the artist-wanderer Everett Ruess wrote to his brother Waldo from Chinle, Arizona, in 1932. "And when the time comes to die, I'll find the wildest, loneliest, most desolate spot there is."

Imagining his final days, Ruess wanted to be far from the mark of man, deep in the silence of the wilderness he adored. Ruess didn't fear dying in the woods. He welcomed an end that would join him forever with the land. What he *didn't* want was for someone to find his body and haul his remains out of the very place that filled his soul with purpose and meaning. His letter to his brother would end up being powerfully prophetic. Ruess vanished without a trace, presumably dying in that wildest, loneliest place, forever under the raven-colored night sky he loved so much.

For me, the loneliest place to die is not a desert or a mountaintop or a cave. It's in your heart, your spirit. It's the place you arrive after years of apathy, of refusing to live your life like a gushing faucet, a crashing wave, an avalanche. It means never being satisfied with stasis, resisting arbitrary rules, setting down your baggage and grabbing at life with both hands and an open heart.

So much has changed since I made my first solo trek into the unknown in 1998, and I've received many gifts in my travels: gifts of kindness, of insight, of friendship, and of challenge. I hope that in some small way this book returns those favors and inspires in you the desire to live the way you want to.

I hope you make a commitment to spend some time alone thinking about what will make your life one that you'll look back on with no regrets. Challenge yourself to do things you never thought you could do. Face your fears. Get back on the horse. Pull that audacious dream you buried into the light of day. Make a commitment to nourish it until it grows into the spectacular thing that will transform you and your life.

At the end of everything, I know I'll look back with no regrets save one: I wish I'd started sooner. Don't let one more minute of the life you dream of remain hidden behind the horizon. Dump your excess baggage, only pack what you can carry, and start out on the path toward that dream.

ACKNOWLEDGMENTS

IN THIS SMALL SPACE it is not possible to thank all the people who have woven themselves into the fabric of my life and influenced the outcome. Gratitude, however, must be publicly acknowledged to the following: my National Geographic team—editor Karen Kostyal, whose patience and insight meant the world to me and a better book for you; researcher Julie Beer, whose cheerful efficiency was always a bright light on sometimes gloomy days; project manager Bridget English; and, of course, VP and Editor in Chief Barbara Brownell Grogan, who showed strong faith in this project even when I had my doubts; my family—Mom, Dad, Shelley, Karen, and Robert—for enduring me; my three extended families—Mark Sr., Mark Jr., and Alexandra Grace Ayers; Ring, Jean-Marie, and Charlton Torrence Jr.; my "sushi mamas," Dr. Ann Hoscheit, Phyllis Wright-Herman, Robyn Strickoff-Forde, Caroline Burrell Macomsen, and Ring; Susan Ratcliff and my sister Girl Scouts; all my friends at Gastonia East Rotary, for helping me love Mondays; Will MacDonald at the *Gaston Gazette,* for the venue to share my adventures with more than just friends and family; Wildacres Retreat in Little Switzerland, North Carolina, where I discovered the heart of this story; the Mountain Writing Workshop at the Banff Centre, for opening a door; mentors Debora Ott and Judith Kohl, two brilliant women who've given more to the world than taken from it; Carrie Miller, sister adventurer; my Just Buffalo writing students, whose trust in me was humbling; Bill and Catherine McGerrigle, because if you're going to travel, you must have really excellent neighbors to watch over what you leave behind; my equine companions Rocky, Farrah, Lover, and Brazen, who have carried me faithfully through life's journey; and T. J. Solomon II, an inspiration to me in all the ways one human being can inspire another.

SELECTED READING

Abbey, Edward. *Desert Solitude: A Season in the Wilderness.* New York: Touchstone, 1990.
[Solitude, Introspection]

Childs, Craig. *The Secret Knowledge of Water: Discovering the Essence of the American Desert.* New York: Back Bay Books, 2001.
[Solitude, Introspection]

Churchill, Winston. *Never Give In! The Best of Winston Churchill's Speeches.* Compiled by Winston S. Churchill. New York: Hyperion, 2004.
[Courage]

Frost, Robert. *The Poetry of Robert Frost.* 2nd rev. ed. Edited by Edward Connery Lathem. New York: Holt Paperbacks, 2002. See esp. "Stopping by Woods on a Snowy Evening."
[Introspection]

Gilbert, Elizabeth. *Eat, Pray, Love.* New York: Viking, 2006.
[Courage, Solitude, Introspection, Commitment]

Gill, Dominic. *Take a Seat: One Man, One Tandem, and Twenty Thousand Miles of Possibilities*. Edinburgh: Mainstream Publishing, 2010.
[Solitude]

Gonzales, Laurence. *Deep Survival: Who Lives, Who Dies, and Why*. New York: W. W. Norton and Company, 2004.
[Courage, Introspection]

Hocking, William Ernest. *Morale and Its Enemies*. New Haven, Conn.: Yale University Press, 1918.
[Courage]

Lansing, Alfred. *Endurance: Shackleton's Incredible Voyage*. 2nd ed. New York: Carroll and Graf, 1999.
[Courage]

Matsuo Basho. *A Haiku Journey: Basho's Narrow Road to a Far Province*. Translated by Dorothy Britton. New York: Kodansha International, 2002.
[Solitude, Introspection]

Matthiessen, Peter. *The Snow Leopard*. New York: Penguin Classics, 2008.
[Introspection]

Miller, William Ian. *The Mystery of Courage*. Cambridge, Mass.: Harvard University Press, 2002.
[Courage]

Mortenson, Greg, and David Oliver Relin. *Three Cups of Tea*. New York: Penguin Books, 2007.
[Courage, Commitment]

Muir, John. *Journeys in the Wilderness*. Edinburgh: Birlinn Limited, 2009.
[Solitude]

————. *My First Summer in the Sierra*. New York: Mariner Books, 1998.
[Solitude]

O'Brien, Tim. *If I Die in a Combat Zone: Box Me Up and Ship Me Home*. New York: Broadway Books, 1999.
[Courage]

Petit, Philippe. *To Reach the Clouds: My High-wire Walk Between the Twin Towers*. London: Faber and Faber, 2004.
[Commitment]

Ralston, Aron. *Between a Rock and a Hard Place*. London: Simon and Schuster UK, 2005.
[Courage]

Roosevelt, Eleanor. *The Autobiography of Eleanor Roosevelt*. Cambridge, Mass.: Da Capo Press, 2000.
[Courage]

————. *You Learn by Living: Eleven Keys for a More Fulfilling Life*. Philadelphia: Westminster Press, 2009.
[Courage]

Rusho, W. L. *Everett Ruess: A Vagabond for Beauty*. Layton, Utah: Gibbs Smith, 1983.
[Solitude]

————. *The Wilderness Journals of Everett Ruess*. Layton, Utah: Gibbs Smith, 1998.
[Solitude]

Scrivener, Leslie. *Terry Fox: His Story*, rev. ed. Toronto: McClelland and Stewart, 2000.
[Commitment]

Shultz, Gladys Denny, and Daisy Gordon Lawrence. *Lady From Savannah: The Life of Juliette Low.* New York: J. B. Lippincott, 1958.
[Courage]

Sogyal Rinpoche. *The Tibetan Book of Living and Dying.* New York: HarperOne, 1994.
[Solitude]

Steinbach, Alice. *Without Reservations: The Travels of an Independent Woman.* New York: Random House, 2000.
[Solitude, Introspection]